The Myth of Mr. Mom

Real Stories by Real Stay-At-Home Dads

Edited by
Jeremy Rodden

Authors
Sonny Lemmons * Christian Jenson
Shawn Scarber * Jeremy Rodden
Toby Tate * Leo Dee
Charlie Andrews * Gerhi Feuren

Published by Portmanteau Press LLC, Chesapeake, VA

Published by:
Portmanteau Press LLC
PO BOX 1411
Chesapeake, VA 23327
http://www.portmanteaupress.com/

ISBN: 978-0-9834253-1-1

Cover design by:
Jennifer Bruck
Cover picture by:
Samantha Rodden

Table of Contents

Popular Culture Propels The Myth Of Mr. Mom

by Jeremy Rodden

Oscar Wilde argued that art demonstrates what will later become accepted as a representation of ideal beauty and thus art is imitated. For the sake of this discussion, replace the concept of beauty with one of culturally acceptable family dynamics, and the point remains the same. Popular culture serves as an example of the general acceptance of cultural changes, whether it is the perception of what is beautiful, or the understanding that men are very capable of being primary caregivers and nurturing homemakers. If Wilde was correct, the rare stay-at-home dad in Western culture is far from being accepted as a normal representation of life.

Popular culture is often a good indicator of how well cultural change has been assimilated into mainstream society. For example, Captain Kirk and Uhura kissing on *Star Trek* in the late 1960's caused a little stir at the time. An interracial kiss would barely cause a ripple in the world today, a sign that interracial couples are not as taboo now as they once were in Western culture. Ted Danson and Whoopi Goldberg certainly didn't cause a big outrage when *Made in America* came out in 1993. Neither did Julia Stiles and Sean Patrick Thomas with 2001's *Save the Last Dance*.

In more recent years, the same trend has been seen in the rise in acceptance of homosexuality in popular culture. While homosexual couples are not as accepted as interracial couples, recent films like *Brokeback Mountain* (2005) and *The Kids are All Right* (2010) explore these relationships in a nonjudgmental way that promotes realistic discussion on the acceptance of this cultural change in modern society. The characters on the television series *Glee* are further helping to normalize homosexuality in pop culture, even amidst controversy.

While these two examples may seem to be much more far-reaching and society-altering examples of changes in Western culture than the subject of this book, men struggling with the stigmas associated with being a stay-at-home father feel their concerns are just as real.

The title of this anthology, *The Myth of Mr. Mom*, is an allusion to the 1983 film, *Mr. Mom*, starring Michael Keaton. As this was one of the first examples of a stay-at-home dad in

Western pop culture, it serves as a harbinger of how stay-at-home dads would be perceived for years. For those who don't know the plot, *Mr. Mom* is the story about a successful automotive engineer who loses his job and has to flip roles with his stay-at-home wife because she is able to find work before he can.

Myth #1: A man staying at home is the result of a lack of options, not a conscious decision by a family.

As he adjusts to this new role, Michael Keaton has hilarious escapades involving his inability to handle basic household tasks such as vacuuming. One of the most famous scenes from the movie is when Keaton resorts to using the hand dryer in the bathroom to dry off his baby's bottom. Further, he doesn't even know how to operate the washer and dryer, leading us to:

Myth #2: Men are incapable of completing even the most basic of household tasks without the aid of a woman.

The story progresses with the main character becoming depressed and distant. He lets himself go physically and wears the same shirt every day. He begins watching soap operas and has strange daydreams about being with a woman other than his wife.

Myth #3: Men who are stay-at-home dads are unhappy with their role and come to resent their circumstances that forced them into the situation.

As Michael Keaton finally gets his bearings and begins becoming an effective stay-at-home father and homemaker, the story focuses more on the problems with the relationship between the two parents. At the end of the movie, he gets his job back at the automotive plant and things return to normal–the "happy" ending.

Myth #4: Men would prefer to work outside the home and the household dynamic can only return to normal if this is the case.

Exploring other examples of stay-at-home dads in popular culture over the last thirty years since *Mr. Mom* was produced, one finds the majority continues to propagate one or all of these myths. *Growing Pains* and *Full House*, two very popular sitcoms in the 1980's, toyed with the idea but they were not real representations of stay-at-home dads.

In *Growing Pains*, the father became a stay-at-home but still worked as a psychiatrist from a home office. In this case, though, the children were already much older and the mother had already been the stay-at-home for what many consider the "hard" years to be an at-home parent. When the show later added a baby, they also added a nanny because, while the father was able to handle the grown children, a baby was just too much.

In *Full House*, the father had to deal with the untimely death of his wife and had three small children to care for. His brother-in-law and best friend moved in to help serve as co-parents to the girls. The show seemed to suggest with some of the comedic moments that even three men combined couldn't handle the tasks of caring for young children. By season two, they added Aunt Becky to the mix to make sure a woman could be there to help the muddling men in raising the children. They sure solved that problem.

In the 2000's, two more popular examples of stay-at-home dads came around. In 2003, the Eddie Murphy film *Daddy Day Care* borrowed a lot of the men-can't-hack-it comedy from previous examples. *Daddy Day Care* presents another visual of a man staying home as a last resort after losing his job, bumbling through basic parenting skills, and being relieved to go back to a *real* job. In this case, at least, the movie ends with Eddie Murphy realizing he preferred staying with the children and he leaves his job to go back to the home and his day care business.

Comedian Bernie Mac explored being a pseudo-stay-at-home dad in *The Bernie Mac Show* early in the decade. He takes custody of his sister's three kids when she enters drug rehab. One positive difference in this example is that Mac shows he is very capable of handling the house and taking care of the kids very early in the show. He does, however, struggle with the title of being a stay-at-home dad and has self-doubts about his manhood because of his new role in life. The show was strongest and most poignant in the episode "Bernie Mac, Ladies Man," where Bernie dealt with this issue head-on and came out confident in his manhood and his role as a primary caregiver.

While *The Bernie Mac Show* was a big step forward in showing that men are capable of taking on the stay-at-home role, some of the myths and stereotypes were still used for jokes. The only example in popular culture of a stay-at-home father not being used as a vehicle for comedy is in the TeleToon cartoon series *Johnny Test*. The fact that gender roles are reversed is not even discussed in the show, outside of an acknowledgement that the mom is a successful professional and the dad is a neat freak.

Now that popular culture has been explored, it is time to get to the meat of this collection. In the following pages, you will read *real* stories by *real* stay-at-home dads. Some of them are quite humorous and some are quite serious, but all of these stories serve to give real-world examples of the struggles stay-at-home fathers face when transitioning into an unfamiliar role, dealing with the difficulties of stay-at-home parenting, and facing the lack of understanding by people on the outside who can't grasp that men are just as capable as women at running a household on a daily basis.

Committing Professional Suicide

by Sonny Lemmons

There are certain events that stand as galvanizing moments in your generation. Events where, no matter your age or how much time has passed since the event happened, you always remember where you were and what you we doing when it occurred: the first manned landing on the moon, the Kennedy assassination, the explosion of the *Challenger*, and the fall of the World Trade Center towers, just to cite a few.

For me, there was the day I announced I was leaving behind a thirteen-year career in higher education administration to become a stay-at-home dad. Perhaps, in comparison, this was not quite as epic in scope as the aforementioned events. To many of my colleagues, it was apparently nearly as unexpected, controversial, and shocking. As I would come to find out during my first year of staying home with my son, other individuals–family, friends, and even perfect strangers–would share this sense of disbelief, horror, and questioning of how this decision shifted their perception of the world around them.

But first: the back-story.

After my wife and I discovered she was pregnant, like many first-time parents, we floated through the first two trimesters somewhat blissfully ignorant of the paradigm shift approaching. We had friends, cousins, and co-workers who had kids, so it's not as if we didn't at least peripherally understand the reality of what was required to take care of a child . . . for a few hours. As we babysat them. Add in to the mix the idea that neither of us knew of a parent–outside of our own mothers–who had stayed or was staying home with their kid. It was obvious what the expected norm was: procreate, daycare, lather, rinse, repeat. After all, that's what all the cool kids were doing. This way, you could have your life cake and eat it, too.

So before the impending arrival of our bundle of joy, we started doing research on a safe and quality daycare. At the time, we were living in Miami, both working for the same university. My wife's position provided us with housing at the university as part of her compensation package, so we were hoping to find someplace relatively close to campus. As luck would have it, there was a daycare facility located literally across the street from the building we worked and lived in. It was about as ideal a situation as we could hope for, and something that other parents told us they would *kill* for: no traffic to fight though at the start or end of the day, if we were running late it's not like it would take long to get there, and God forbid something should happen to him or he get sick, we could literally be there in under five minutes.

The grueling application and interview process didn't phase us in the least bit. The "sticker shock" of discovering that every month we would be paying what felt like the GDP of some countries was tough to swallow, but we got over it relatively quickly. Again: this was the "norm." This was what we knew that everyone else who had kids did and was expected to do. I mean, what was the alternative?

The singular eye-opening moment that made us stop dead in our tracks and question if we were making the right choice for him and not just the right choice for us was when we sat down and objectively did a time management analysis. My wife's position called for a lot of "non-traditional" office hours, often skewing late into the night and on the weekends. My position was more traditional in terms of the office hours it required, but there were a number of expectations that fell under the catchall designation of "Other Duties As Assigned" that caused me to work nights and weekends as well.

When we charted out that on a *good* week, provided that there were no emergencies to respond to, no last-minute programs to assist with, and no late-night staff or student organization meetings to attend, we discovered that we *might* spend two to three hours–maximum–a day with him. On average. Now, were we to factor in feeding, bathing, and diaper times, this number would have increased, but not substantially. We were trying to ascertain the amount of time we would have bonding as a family. What we discovered was that the amount of quality waking hours we would share with him was less than the average amount of time we might spend on any given evening just sitting in front of our television set.

This revelation kind of made the notion of effectively paying someone to raise him seem . . . obscene. To have spent nine months getting him ready for the world, only to be born and then turned over to other people to raise–mostly in school–for the better part of the next two decades? To have someone else probably experience the milestones–first step, first word, first crappy attitude from cutting his first tooth–that should have been ours to celebrate? Not that my wife and I base all our major life decisions from what we've seen on television, but I knew from *Lost* the dangers of letting our child be "raised by another."

So, we made the only choice that made sense. The one that flew in the face of conventional wisdom and logic. The choice that was right for *us*. Since my wife's job provided us with a place to live, and trying to find a house or apartment on top of having a kid born at the same time seemed a little extreme to try and manage, I would quit my job and stay home with him. Yes, this was going to drop us to a one-income family, but placing him in daycare would also have basically done the same thing. We understood that there would have to be some sacrifices involved on our part, but weighing those "losses" against what we stood to lose in terms of memories and time spent with him made them seem as trite and materialistic as they actually were.

Now, bear in mind that I had genuinely, literally never spent more than three hours at a stretch with a child of *any* age before this. I had never changed a diaper in my life. I barely knew how to entertain myself most of the time, let alone a baby. *"But,"* I humorously thought, *"I have a Master's degree. I am an intelligent, educated man, and I have managed to survive for nearly 40 years on this planet. How difficult can this really be?"* Little did I recall that I also used to believe that an imaginary mouse lived in the bricks under the oven in my parent's house, so denial and delusions are something I am clearly intimately familiar with. Yet despite my inexperience, my wife and I were at peace with our decision. We knew that this would be a far more ideal scenario for him–someone who loved and cared for him would be overseeing his development and serving as his caregiver It would be a great chance for him to not only bond with me, but also to be able to see a male serving in the role which shatters gender stereotypes–something he would not have encountered in daycare, as *every* employee at the one we were considering was female.

The "fun"–and I use that term in the most sarcastic way imaginable–came when we began to let others in on our decision.

I discussed the possibility of quitting my job with my supervisor well before I submitted my resignation. He was skeptical that I actually would leave until the day I gave my notice. After all, I was working in a position that had all but been created *for* me at the university. It was a great stepping-stone for me to potentially be launched into bigger and better things within my division. It offered me opportunities to flex my creative and administrative muscles. It drew upon my years of professional experience, highlighting my strengths, providing me opportunities to grow and network with individuals who could assist in guiding me into an ideal professional future. Ideal insomuch as I was willing to make the job, and not my family, a priority.

I do need to mention that before my wife and I pulled the trigger on me leaving my job, we did not make this decision in a vacuum. We sought out the advice, opinions, and general feedback from close friends and colleagues who we thought could help us to sort through the haze of what it really might be like for me to quit, and possibly help us see any potential hazards we had not considered. I had stayed in contact with many of my professors from both my undergraduate and graduate school days, so I thought who better to assist me with a little career guidance than those who had helped me before? So, I sent emails to a select few, asking for their thoughts.

Bear in mind that both my wife and I knew we were not going to stay in Miami forever, and eventually, we would conduct a nationwide job search again. We knew that whichever of us found a position we were truly passionate about, provided that it was a financially feasible move, we would strike out for the unknown together. Whether this meant that I would continue in my role as a stay-at-home dad, my wife would swap out with me and stay home with him for a while, or he might be old enough to start preschool at the time was an unknown.

It was this same "X factor" that caused one of my former professors to come close to losing it when she called me to express her opinion about me quitting my job. According to her, I had worked too hard and too long to just throw away my future like this. My career trajectory was apparently poised on this amazing tipping point, and to leave it all behind was, in her words, "committing professional suicide." In her opinion, no potential employer would give my resume a second glance, especially since I would be intentionally causing a gap in my employment dates. To have such an "unprofessional excuse"–again, her words–for leaving was inexcusable and no employer would take me seriously. After all, if I left once, doesn't that just set up a dangerous precedent that I might leave again, inferring that I am not committed to my employer?

Because clearly, no parent, regardless of gender, has ever set their family as a higher priority than their job. Ever.

Despite her warnings–and after taking my former professor's name off of our Christmas card list, I proceeded with my choice to stay home with my son. My wife and I timed my final two weeks at my office to dovetail into her coming off of maternity leave/the end of the summer break, so that there was still a buffer period before the beginning of the fall semester and the arrival of students. Although it was going to put a mild strain on the workloads of my colleagues until they replaced me, my supervisor at least understood the "why" of why I was leaving.

The reactions from my coworkers were far more interesting. Understandably, some were a bit upset, the aforementioned "mild strain" being their primary reason to grouse. Some were relieved I was leaving, as we had never really gotten along all that well in the first place. However, one of my coworkers expressed an opinion which in many ways became this quasi-prophetic utterance of misunderstanding which came back to not only chip away at my confidence level during the first few weeks of me as a stay-at-home dad, but also served as the point of view that I'm certain many people thought but were, unlike her, too tactful to just blurt out loud:

"I can understand why your wife might want to stay home, since she's his mother, and as women we're made to want to take care of our children. But men aren't nurturing. How are you going to know what to do with him?"

My gut instinct to respond to her was to either just stare at her with a look that would have lowered the temperature in our conference room to 17 degrees Celsius, or to roll my eyes and blurt out, "Holy crap, you've seen through my ploy to be able to just drop him into his swing while I sit at home in my underwear, drink beer, and watch ESPN all day. Please don't tell my wife."

After spending a few moments in a fantasy, which involved me keying her car after work, I decided to be the adult in the scenario and tell her, "You know, I *don't* know. And that's going to be part of the fun, figuring it all out on this journey with him." Like many men–or to be fair, like many *parents*, regardless of gender–when I first started considering what I would do while I was home with my kid, I had a false sense of the ease in which this might go. After all, the first couple of months would, in comparison to later years, be relatively uncomplicated: feed, change, nap, tummy time, stroll around campus, and on and on in an endless cycle of early development activities. Even though I cognitively understood the rigor of the ritual and constant routine of feeding him day in and out at all hours, I didn't quite grasp the physical or emotional toll it might take on me.

Never was this better illustrated than in the social jungle of meeting and mingling at a function. If you've never stopped to consider this before, odds are that when you meet someone for the first time, after introducing yourself and getting your conversational partner's name, you start out by asking them the low-impact question: "So, what do you do for a living?" Men are by and large more apt to let this be our leading question, partially because we tend to identify ourselves through one of two lenses: family and career. Nothing was more unsettling and apparently had the ability to end a conversation with me better than when I dropped the "I'm a stay-at-home dad" bomb into the exchange. I honestly have had a number of people just stare at me, slack-jawed, and unable to even come back with something more intelligent than "Oh, well. That's . . . wow. Yeah." Once, I even had one woman, after informing me she was a visiting professor from an ivy-league university, just look at me with a polite grin half-frozen on her face before turning her back on me, without blinking, to strike up a conversation with a person standing behind her.

It is interesting to note that nowadays, since I have taken on some freelance paid writing and editing assignments, the stigma of me as a stay-at-home dad to some people has changed a bit. People seem far more comfortable with me saying that I *work* from home instead of saying I *just* stay at home to take care of my son. To be fair, the work I do is mainly done during his nap times, at nights and on the weekends, so my volume of work–and corresponding paycheck–is negligible. But the simple fact that I am somewhat adhering to the social construct of "man as financial provider" makes my being at home, dressing in jeans or shorts all the time, and only shaving every three days seem less bohemian and easier to swallow.

It's fascinating when you stop to consider that even as recent as the 1970's, if a stay-at-home mom sought to bring in an outside or additional income–from selling cosmetics, plastic food containers or the like–it was generally frowned upon. After all, didn't this take time away from her cooking, cleaning, taking care of the kids, or other essential domestic responsibilities? If so, how is there a double standard that states men who work from home are somehow more responsible than those who exclusively spend all their time and energy as the primary caregiver?

Regardless of if I was being paid in money from a publisher or smiles from my son, my lack of full time employment outside the home was still unsettling to a number of people who simply could not process the idea that I would willingly elect to be with my son all the time.

It didn't end there; I cannot even calculate the number of times I have been stopped by total strangers while out shopping, at the park, at a museum, or wherever who comment to me and my son on how nice it is that daddy is taking the day/afternoon off to spend time with him, or is taking him so "mommy can catch a break." I can't begin to express how many times at the pediatrician's or dentist's offices the staff have remarked about how "good" I am with him because I was - and I quote from one experience - "paying attention to him." I don't know what they thought was going to happen, that I was going to Tweet about the experience at the time instead of trying to help calm him and get him to settle down?

To be fair, I *have* seen a number of moms who, when they are out with their kids, have their noses buried in their Blackberry or iPhone. But more than making a critical statement on how over-dependent our culture has become on social media, what these nurses were saying–and by extension, inferring also from the comments of strangers in public–people expect for fathers to be not as connected with their kids as mothers are. I'm not sure if this is due in part to the growing number of absentee fathers found in families across the country or it's because the majority of television shows and movies portray dads as lovable and well-meaning but ultimately ineffectual goofballs who only through a comedy of trails and errors manage to be even remotely capable at taking care of children.

It was partially because of this misconception–coupled with all the helpful advice and judgments lobbed against me–that I could feel my confidence as a stay-at-home parent eroding: *was* I capable of doing this?

It's not as if there are a number of resources available in print that I could fall back on for ideas or encouragement; the majority of the parenting books I researched before staying home with my son either dealt with advice on how to morally raise a child once they were past the toddler age, or else they were so basic and elementary in their structure and content that they were honestly a little insulting. I was raised under the gender construct that I was supposed to be the "breadwinner" in my family, so I also began to feel . . . less manly, for lack of a better phrase. Since I was motivated out of a self-imposed false sense of guilt that I was "just" a stay-at-home parent and not contributing anything financially to the equation, I began to feel the need to prove (or "*over*-prove") myself to the naysayers and questioners that I could just as capably and just as competently do this.

I do need to go on record to say that at no point did my wife *ever* join the chorus of deriders. If anything, she stood on the opposite side of the fence, encouraging me to do *less* around the house. Case in point: once we progressed past the point where rice cereal was the main dietary staple, I decided to take it upon myself to make my son's food. All of it. So, we utilized a leftover gift card from our wedding and bought a high-end baby food cooker and gourmet baby food cookbook. Yes, I did begin to feel a little holier-than-thou when I would see other parents feeding their kid Brand X jar food and our son was eating steamed organic, fair-trade carrots with ginger seasoning. I also developed ODD, Obsessive Domestic Disorder, and began to do all the laundry, do all the cleaning, and buy all the groceries and supplies. My wife was coming in from a hard day at work, and she just needed to relax and rest, right? Not deal with such mundane chores or responsibilities, right?

I was one pearl necklace away from turning into Jim, not June, Cleaver.

For my own sanity–as well as because I needed to understand I had nothing to prove to anyone–I needed to start to get comfortable in my own stay at home skin. Just because I was literally carrying our kid everywhere by myself did not mean I had to carry the entire weight of responsibility of our house by myself. My kid was happy and healthy, and neither of us had managed to drink mercury, eat Styrofoam, sit in the corner all day and lick our feet, or do whatever it was people might have thought my "non-nurturing" self might have done with him. My *"job"* was no longer a career. It was now a legacy. For as unconventional as it may have seemed to some, it's been the most rewarding thing I've ever done.

The past three years have been fraught with ups and downs, good days and bad. To be honest, there have been times when I have stared longingly at the dress shirts and ties slowly turning from modern style to vintage in my closet and have missed being in an office. I have had detractors: one guy I have not seen in over 20 years sent me a string of messages on Facebook to explain to me how I was operating outside of God's design for my life as a husband and father - but that's another story. I have had doubters. I have also had supporters. Cheerleaders. I have made friends with other stay-at-home dads–I'm *not* the only guy doing this, who knew?–stay-at-home moms, and I have had the continual, unconditional love and support from the two most important people in this equation: my wife Ashley and my son Malakai.

I'm just thankful none of my previous performance evaluations involved as many hugs as this one does.

About The Author

Sonny Lemmons likes to refer to himself as a "writer of stuff." He left a 13-year career in Higher Education Administration specializing in counseling, staff training, and leadership development to be a stay-at-home dad three years ago. He views this as his best career move yet. His blog Looking Through the Windshield (www.lookthrough.net) documents his journey of questions about faith and fatherhood, with the occasional *Doctor Who* reference thrown in for good measure. He's probably drinking coffee as you read this. His wife (Ashley) and son (Malakai) love him, but don't really get his sense of humor, either.

Mr. Mom; A Retrospective

by Christian Jensen

"Come on son, time to wake up."

Something akin to a zombie's growl emits from under the sheets, allowing me to zero in on the boy's head. I reach down and grab the covers, tugging them gently.

"It's time for school. You need to get up." It's six thirty in the morning, sunlight barely squeezing over the horizon. I've been up for two hours, writing. My youngest son and I go to bed at the same time. He's thirty years younger than I am. Why can't he wake up on time, just once?

The zombie growl turns into a whine. That's it. I yank the covers up and roll them around my arm, effectively creating a giant boxing glove, before reaching down and grabbing an exposed leg. Yanking the child off the bed with one hand I repeatedly pummel him about the head and neck with the covers until his whine turns into a giggle.

"You have one minute to get downstairs." I make my voice really deep at this point, so I sound like I actually have some kind of authority over him. "Or I'll pull your underwear over your head and give you an atomic wedgie." With the threat out in the open and the boy flailing around the bed screaming something about me being creepy, I head out of his room, victorious.

One down. Two to go.

My mornings are all the same. I wake up at 4:30 and head downstairs, eyes closed and face aimed towards the smell of coffee. Once I pour and drink the first cup, I light the day's first cigarette and finish off the second cup while I boot up the computers. I'm not sure if people still boot up computers, but that's how I think about it. They whir and whine and make noises while I whimper and curse myself for getting out of bed so fucking early.

With cigarette and coffee both dead, I lurch into the kitchen for another cup, then sit down and watch the cursor for a few minutes until I figure out what the hell I was working on yesterday. Once I have some semblance of order I begin to write, usually falling into a good groove and pounding out my goal of 2500 words before the wife jumps in the shower at 6:30.

Hearing the shower go on means I can have one more cigarette and play on social media for fifteen minutes before I need to unleash the Kraken. Unfortunately that isn't a sexual euphemism in regards to my manhood; it's how I think about waking up my youngest. He's the evil one–the cranky and ill tempered opposite of a morning person. If flames could shoot out of his eyes, or I was foolish enough to let him sleep with a loaded gun–I'll only make *that* mistake once–he would shoot me in the crotch and giggle while I flailed, begging for mercy.

My two oldest, ages fourteen and twelve, are much easier.

"Wake up." I say to my oldest son. He then wakes up.

"Wake up." I say to my middle son. He then screams at me to get out of his room, falls out of his bed and unleashes a torrent of obscenities no twelve year old should know while struggling to untangle his chunky frame from the covers. Then he wakes up.

Now that I have put myself at great bodily risk and awoken my hell-spawn, I head into the kitchen where I make them a healthy breakfast. I spend the next fifteen minutes cooking oatmeal, baking biscuits, slicing fruit, toasting bread and the like. By the time it's done and my kids are all sitting in front of the

TV like the brain-dead idiots they are, I'm ready to serve them. I deliver the nutritious, homemade meal.

Then they ask for cereal.

After a string of obscenities from me, the likes of which no middle-aged man should know, my children kindly relent. They eat what's in front of them, devouring everything but the plates, all the while complaining that cereal is easier and tastes better. By this time I am on my fifth cup of coffee and the nicotine in my system is wearing out, and the urge to kill is growing strong.

Then the wife comes down.

"Make sure you call the doctor and get the boys prescriptions refilled, and be sure to tell him to call the pharmacy and then pick it up before you get them from school. There is *so* much laundry. You should get to work on that. My car needs to be inspected andthedogsaredueforthiershotsandfindoutwhe nregistrationisforwrestlingandareyougoingtoco achthisyearandwhenisyourcheckforthelastboo

kgoingtogethereineedtopaythecarinsurance . .
."

I don't know what she says because I don't really listen, yet somehow I manage to get everything on her list done, plus mow the lawn and handle all the car issues that come up, as well as any home-repair projects.

The wife gets dressed and eats her breakfast while I make lunches for the kids, placing every sandwich and snack in a brown paper bag. We have the insulated kind that keeps the cold stuff cold, but I like using plain, old-fashioned brown paper bags, so I can write embarrassing things on them.

"Have a great day at school, DADDY WUBS U!"

"Don't' let the mean boys hurt your feelings. Remember: YOU'RE SPECIAL!"

"Don't tell anyone about that rash. THEY'LL NEVER KNOW!"

"Hey, at least your MOM kinda likes you."

"Sorry, you're NOT adopted."

I stuff their lunches into backpacks, tell them all to have a good day and push them out the door. After locking, dead-bolting and nailing the door shut I laugh maniacally. They're gone. They're really, really gone. *Mwahahahahahaha!*

It's time for cup of coffee number six, cigarette number three and some music.

As I walk around the house, usually in my boxers and worn-out robe, I begin to talk to the only captive audience that gives a shit about what I have to say: my dogs. I have a Great Dane, a German Shepherd/Lab mix, a Jack Russell, and something my father adopted–a tiny little hairball that's cute as a button, if you find buttons cute, that I inherited when he died. It's a motley group, but they love me and enjoy my company. Plus I feed them, so I'm the man. They listen while I talk, follow me around the house while I clean and lie around me as I write.

Now that my day has officially begun and the family is off doing things, I work. By that I mean playing on social media for a while, plugging my books and replying to comments on my blog, answering emails and the like before getting up and doing the breakfast dishes. After whirling through the kitchen like a buff, tattooed cyclone–which is going to be inscribed on my tombstone, now that I've thought of it–I go through the rest of the house picking up laundry and straightening up. Nothing has to be perfect yet, because I clean in stages.

Stage 1: Kitchen and general pick up. Laundry. Pull out dinner to thaw.

Once that's done I sit down and write for another hour and a half, trying to get an additional 2500 words done. Then it's another half hour of social media

Stage 2: Bathrooms and upstairs. Laundry. Make marinade, if applicable, for dinner.

Now it's usually around 9:00 by the time I get this stage done. Still plenty early and I have the whole day ahead of me. This is where things start to collapse. I'm hungry and so wired from having seven or eight cups of coffee that I can't concentrate to write. I need to eat, but cooking for the family and then cleaning their dishes has left me unable to decide what to eat. If I baked muffins, then I shovel a few of them down my throat. If not, I usually have the cereal I won't let my kids eat.

Then I need to get busy writing again, doing another hour until the laundry is done, then doing another load and going back to writing until that load is done. Then it's another load and social media until noon.

Noon is nice. I sit down with a sandwich or some other lunch-type food and watch TV. I shut off the brain, eat and drink something without caffeine, usually Jolt Cola or Mountain Dew. I eat healthy, so it only makes sense that I drink like shit. If it's not alcoholic then it's chocked full of caffeine. And sugar. Sometimes I think it would be healthier if I drank crack, but that would be *WAY* too expensive.

So I get my rest for half an hour while I eat lunch and watch TV. No kids to argue or fight with, no housework or writing to do, no editing or social media. No thinking. It's like a mini vacation. Or talking to my wife. Both require absolutely *no* brain function.

Then it's back to work, which means more laundry and more writing until 1:30. By then my back is an intricate collection of knots that screams when I move, reminding me that I *really* need to get back to the gym. Sure, maybe I can fit going to the gym in place of sleep. That would be *awesome.* Because sometimes 6 hours is just waaayyy too much.

Now I shower, which should be relaxing, but isn't. Because I can't just stop writing exactly at 1:30 I usually go over, so the shower has to be rushed. Soap is a luxury anyway, and shampoo is for pussies. Let the water hit you while you're naked and standing up, and it's technically a shower. Now I run into my bedroom naked and pick out whatever clothes I can find. If I look stupid and embarrass my kids, then I win ten points.

So wearing my plaid shorts and Thomas the Tank Engine T-shirt–two sizes too small, thank you very much–is completely acceptable, provided that I put on black socks and sandals before heading out the door. If its winter I just put long johns underneath the shorts and a bright yellow coat, and some kind of wool hat with things hanging off it that make me look like a rooster. Now I rush to my truck and proceed to speed through three other school zones before getting to my kids. We *had* to pick Catholic school.

I'm always punctual to get my kids because my mother never was. Have you ever been the last kid picked up at school in the seventies? You either got some guy in a trench coat calling himself Uncle Steve and asking you if you wanted to meet something in his pants called "Puff the Magic Dragon," or you had some long-haired kid in overly tight plaid pants and matching paisley shirt asking you if you wanted to try something in the back of his van called "Puff the Magic Dragon." Either way having a late parent is horrible, so I'm always on time.

On time really means early, so I get there and stand in the parking lot, waiting for the kids to be released. Most other parents talk to one another, but I hate all the other parents. If I told most of them that I write horror and erotica for a living their heads would swell up and explode, raining confetti and snickers bars down on the rest of us. Then they would rush home and secretly buy all the erotica I've ever written, touching themselves while they sit in their closets reading and crying as they whisper things like "Puff the Magic Dragon, where did you go?" So needless to say I simply tell people that I'm unemployed, because it's less embarrassing than telling them I'm a writer.

*Author's Note: I'm actually *incredibly* proud to be making a living as a writer. I pick and choose who I tell I'm a writer, not because of pride or fear of being condescended to, but because I have a violent temper and don't want to go back to jail. Ever. Seriously, you punch a priest *once...*

Finally, school lets out and the kids rush into the parking lot. Some are crying, some anxious to get home, others in foul moods and obviously cranky. Almost all of them need a nap and a snack. I'm talking about the parents. The kids are just happy to get out of prison for the next eighteen hours or so.

I pick up my kids and chat about their day, getting them into the truck and asking about homework and tests during our half hour drive home. Then I give them a small list of chores and remind them to please hang up their clothes.

While I'm picking up their clothes, they do homework, then finish chores, and then disappear. I have no idea where they actually go to, but it's somewhere with an X-Box. The house could catch on fire and our dogs explode into flaming hairballs, and they wouldn't get off that fucking machine. And I love it. I sacrifice virgins and goats to the X-Box gods, because that is my most favorite time of all.

You see, while the kids do homework and chores I cook dinner. Healthy, everything from scratch, absolutely delicious, dinner. When they disappear to X-Box land I have *nothing to do*. The house is clean, writing is done, dinner is cooking, and the homework is finished. My day is complete, and I can sit down with a book and read.

Then the wife comes home.

I need to be careful, because if she walks in the door and I am sitting there with a book in my hand she will assume I did nothing, and then the nit picking begins. If, however, she comes home and I am covered in flour and sawdust and blood, rebuilding an interior wall while speaking with my editor on the phone and battling an escaped lobster, than it's all good. She gives me a kiss, whimpers about how horrible her day was and then proceeds to tell me exactly how stupid everyone in her office is. I pretend to listen while checking on dinner and making her a plate.

At this point in my day I often wonder if I sounded the same when I was working and she stayed home. It's nice to remember a time when the roles were reversed and I was out there in the "real world," leaving the house early and heading to a job, interacting with people and being a productive member of society. Those memories are great, because it reminds me exactly why I never want to do that again.

About The Author

Christian Jensen is a horror and erotica author living in the wilds of central Jersey. He has been writing for over 20 years, and currently has over 25 books available on Kindle, Nook, and Smashwords.

His Blog: Beautiful Stories for Ugly Children has received rave reviews and is updated constantly with FREE works of short fiction, as well as links to his work, reviews, other publications with his writing, and news about the author.

http://horrorwritingdaddy.blogspot.com

He is active on twitter: @hororwritindad.

You can always reach him via e-mail.

He loves to communicate with his readers: MSSProductions@verizon.net.

Project: New Dad

by Shawn Scarber

It was near the end of July, one of the hottest months of the year in Texas, and my ten-year-old daughter and I had spent every evening in our apartment swimming pool. We usually started with laps. We would occasionally race. Sometimes she beat me and sometimes she let me win. We could both feel the tension as the difficult part of our month together drew closer. I knew in the next few days she would return to a home she wasn't happy living in, and I would have to let her go.

Neither of us wanted the month to end. We swam until the sun set and talked about continuing our visits to the pool until the water was too cold to stand, even though we knew we only had a few more days together.

My daughter and I had often talked about what life would be like if she lived with me. I'd told her for years, if living with me was something she wanted, I would do everything in my power to make it happen, but there were no guarantees. I was always open to the discussion, and during that month the topic came up often.

I'd heard stories that she was put in charge of watching her sisters while her mother slept all day. She had told me of long fights between her mother and stepfather. The year before her grades had gone from an average of A's and B's to almost failing certain subjects. I knew something wasn't quite right with her home environment, but I wasn't sure if warranted a trip to court and a long custody battle.

While having breakfast at our favorite diner, I told her to make a list of all the pros and cons of living with me. I explained to her what pros and cons were and told her to think hard about what goes on this list. She told me she would and set to writing. Once she had the list I told her to keep it and think about it another day. I wanted her to be able to consider what she had written, to make sure she was being fair to herself and everyone involved. The next day she came to me and said, she thought her life would be better off if she lived with me. I said I would do everything I could to make that happen.

I knew this wasn't an easy commitment. A friend and I had just moved into a large three-bedroom apartment close to her work. I work from home, so location normally isn't a problem for me, but I had been living in a less than desirable apartment complex and was ready for the change. We were planning out our lives with the idea that my daughter would just be an occasional roommate. This decision wouldn't just affect my life; I had to consider her other family's lives as well. I knew her mother wouldn't be happy with the choice, but what about her step-father, her sisters, her other extended family members? That night I laid in bed thinking of all the changes it would mean to our collective lives. I hadn't even thought to write my own list of pros and cons.

Now I have to reveal a little about myself. I'm a bit nerdy. I'm a computer programmer by trade and I write science fiction as a hobby. If you need to know a second edition D&D rule, I can probably recall it and give you the page number. Like most nerds, I like projects. This just seemed like another difficult project. I would map it out and plan what would come next. I knew there was a pretty good chance I wouldn't be able to get custody of my daughter. Judges aren't keen on taking a child from a family environment and placing the child in the home a single parent. Unless there was just blatant abuse, which didn't seem evident, there wasn't much chance of my plan succeeding. But I had to give it a try.

Then there was one of those incredible coincidences that you would only find in a work of fiction, because no one would believe such a thing could happen in real life. The next day I learned from my daughter's stepfather that he and my daughter's mother would soon be divorcing. I called my daughter's mother to confirm this and we discussed our child's future. We determined that a co-parenting arrangement with me as the primary custodial parent was the best solution for everyone. I had a long talk with my daughter about this and she agreed to the arrangement her mother and I had discussed. I called my lawyer and we put all the necessary legal steps in place to turn what my daughter and I had been discussing as a possibility into a reality.

This is about the time I started hearing all of the congratulations.

Why do people want to constantly congratulate a good father? Is it really such a rarity in our culture? You don't hear many people say, "You're such a good mother," because good mothering is the accepted norm. Does that mean that bad fathering is the accepted norm as well? I worry over these questions, because I fear our society and my culture have set the bar too low. I worry I'm not enough to be a complete set of parents for my daughter, because for good or bad, that's the situation I find myself in. I am a stay-at-home, work-from-home, single father.

I don't believe people gave this praise to erode my confidence as a parent. I saw this praise, not as a means to lift my spirits, but as a comment on the overall status of fatherhood. Everyone had such a poor opinion of fatherhood; I worried that maybe I shouldn't strive to be a great dad, but an adequate mother. Knowing now that a mother figure would be absent from my daughter's life, I started considering what it takes to be both.

What would I need to do to be a good mother and father?

Reading essays on being a single parent, it also became obvious that most of these articles assumed the person reading was a mother. There were far more essays on how a woman can basically fulfill the role of a father, but very few covering the opposite. I researched the big things that mothers bring to the table. The biggest seemed to be the role of nurturer. Apparently, as fathers, that's not one of our strong points.

What? Really? Guys can't be nurturers? Was that true? It was this sort of thinking that plagued me. Perhaps these essays were right. Maybe a mother is more important to a child's life than the father?

I raise all these questions; because I fell prey to a few of these stereotypes when I suddenly found myself the primary custodial parent of my child. I had never worried about my fathering skills in the past, but with the prospect of being the main parental figure in my daughter's life I had to honestly assess my skill set. What if I wasn't good enough for this? What if I couldn't fulfill the role of a father and mother? What if I wasn't nurturing? Oh my God, what does nurturing actually mean? Maybe the stereotypes were true. Maybe I wasn't cut out for this. Would I one day look in the mirror and see Homer Simpson staring back at me?

I had never questioned my fathering skills in the past. My idea of fatherhood involved being a good provider, a protector, and a strong figure capable of giving moral guidance. I had been a weekend father for years. When my daughter stayed with me I tried to fill our time together with life enriching activities that involved trips to the zoos, movies, art and history museums, and time with friends and family. These seemed the important life lessons I needed to impart.

I hadn't considered that when she came to live with me there would be a transition from the fun weekend parent to the not-so-fun homework, chore-assigning, and get-to-bed-on-time parent. Yeah, things would have to change–for her and for me.

However, I decided I wasn't going to allow myself to fall prey to stereotypes. This new arrangement wasn't going to make either of our lives worse, but even better. If learning what nurturing actually means is a part of my new parental identity, then so be it.

As hard as it would be, I would have to let go of some of that old father and embrace the new. They say the first part of a journey is packing, and now I felt packed and ready to get on board, but I had no idea how to arrive at the destination. How would I go from the old dad to this new dad, especially with the limited contact she would now have with her mother? As of this moment, she only sees her mother a couple of hours every week. She doesn't stay weekends with her yet and there doesn't seem to be much of a chance for that in the near future. I worried that trying to take this one alone would make me a worse parent, not better.

Again, I approached the whole process as a project. Yes, there's that nerd part of me again. With enough planning and thought the project would run smoothly and efficiently. Before long, Old Dad could quickly and easily transition into New Dad.

As I wondered what it might take to transition to this new dad, I had a lot of daily living tasks to accomplish first. Yes, like most nerds, I like task lists as well. I lived far enough away from her old home that my daughter had to transfer to a school closer to my apartment. This was the first big negative. She didn't want to transfer to a new school. All her friends were at her old school. Her best friend since first grade was at her old school. I tried to get my daughter to see the bright side. This was an opportunity and there would be a new set of friends. At her old school, she had behavior problems. I wasn't sure if this was because of the instability of her home life or because of the influence of the other kids in her class, but I'd hoped she would see this shift as a chance to clear away those bad habits.

I realized that this new arrangement would involve a lot of compromise, not just on my part, but on her part as well. The new, improved dad would need to realize that this was not a one-way street. We were both making big changes in our lives to make this work.

This time period also made me thankful for the flexibility of my work-at-home programming job. My daughter and I probably spent most of the day traveling to her old school for paperwork, her doctor's office for shot records, and her new school for registration. For anyone who hasn't stood in the long line on school registration day, just think back to the horror stories of old Soviet Russia. It's about the same. Oh, and of course teachers and staff asked about the whereabouts of mom.

We managed to get her registered with only a few hiccups. My daughter did an excellent job of embracing the new opportunities this change would give her. She learned the new bus route, and in a few weeks she had the whole routine of waking, dressing, and being at the corner on time. She even managed to make a friend from a neighboring apartment complex to meet every morning. It seemed the first big challenge was conquered.

Now the old dad liked to go out to eat a lot. In fact, on our weekends together, we normally went out for breakfast, grabbed lunch at a sub shop, and then had a big dinner at a steak house or sushi restaurant. This obviously wasn't something new dad could continue. We discussed our options, and I was surprised to learn that my daughter was pretty open to trying new foods and really liked the idea of cooking and eating at home.

On one of our first nights together we cooked stir-fry. I have one of those huge electric woks that I inherited from a roommate. We bought our fresh ingredients from the local Whole Foods. While in the kitchen, my daughter was excited about the new adventure. She asked if she could cut the vegetables. I said, "Sure. You know to do that?" She said she had done it before when helping her mother cook. So I handed her a sharp knife, gave her the obligatory, "Be careful," and pointed her to the cutting board. She washed and chopped the veggies like a pro.

The meal was a success and she's helped with many meals since that night. We still occasionally go out for dinner or order in from our favorite Chinese food take out, but for the most part we cook healthy and nutritious dinners at home.

Next, we had to work out bedtime. We knew she had to get up early for the bus, but she had been used to staying up late. We talked, and I told her it was important that I have some time to myself. Sure, I'm actually home all day, but that's work time. I'm on the clock. I can usually get laundry done, dishes loaded, and run a few errands, but for the most part I'm working from seven thirty in the morning until well past five in the evening. I used to write fiction in the evenings. I was ready to greatly reduce my writing time in the evening if I had to, but I didn't want to give it up. We came to an understanding that she needed to be in her room by nine. She didn't have to go to sleep, but that was a time for preparing for the next school day, reading, playing the Nintendo, or writing in her journal. She's been pretty good at sticking with our agreement.

Project: New Dad seemed less like an actual project. I guess I'm lucky that my kid and I are pretty compatible. At this very moment, while I sit putting the finishing touches on this essay, we're sitting in a coffee shop in South Dallas. She's playing Zelda on her 3DS and I'm writing this essay on my iPad. That's the thing about projects–they take effort. We seem to be more in the mode of easing into an effortless existence. We're no longer just focused on making daily life work; we're making plans for the future. Where are we going to go on vacation next? What should we do for dinner next week? Are we going to the movies tonight or just going home to read and relax? Something happened while we worked through our daily life's task list.

Something I would say was miraculous, but it was hardly noticeable. I guess things that are hardly noticeable can be miraculous.

She changed. She started to relax. I knew the transition for my daughter wasn't going to be an easy one. It had been a transition she and I had talked about on many occasions, but nothing could have prepared her for it. She had come from an environment where she could never be sure of anything. Life for her had been a guessing game and I think she had expected more of the same living with me, but it wasn't.

We had built our little schedules and rituals. Through the ordinary chores of daily life we had built a new level of trust. It wasn't that she hadn't trusted me before, but I was just someone who she occasionally talked to on the phone or saw on the weekends. I wasn't really even as much a dad as her stepfather. I can understand why she might not trust that everything was going to work out.

As my daughter let go of her worries and started to enjoy her new life, I watched her improve in math, make new friends, and open up. She had her first sleepover with a girl from school. We planned a Halloween party, made invitations, and found the exact costume she wanted. We started a new ritual. Now every day when she comes home from school she has to give me a hug and I congratulate her on surviving another day of school.

As for me, I feel like I've managed to transition to the new dad, but he isn't anything like what I first imagined. Thank goodness. There's no way I could handle managing my life and my relationship with my daughter like a project. I think I've learned what nurturing means. Nurturing is opening your life to your kids. Nurturing is spending the time and putting in the effort despite work, laundry, dinner, and all the other mundane tasks of daily life. Nurturing is being there.

About The Author

Shawn Scarber is an applications developer for one of the leading preventive healthcare companies in the United States, writes science fiction, fantasy and horror, and attended and graduated from Clarion West in 2006. He lives in Dallas, Texas with his daughter, a precocious ginger cat, and a wonderful housemate who also shares in his addiction of really bad reality television.

No, I'm Not Babysitting

by Jeremy Rodden

"Oh, so you're babysitting today?" asked the convenience store clerk, a pleasant smile on her face.

I looked up at her, an infant-filled car seat cradled in the crook of my arm. I wanted to pick up my can of Monster Energy Drink and throw it at her, but I knew she meant no harm. It was not her fault that modern society had such low expectations of fathers that a man with an infant is assumed to be "babysitting" as opposed to a primary caregiver. I smile and respond, "Yes, every day."

When our first son was born in 2005, my wife and I had a tremendous amount of support from our family in taking care of him. I was working as a store manager for a large video game retailer and she was still in medical school. Between coordinating my schedule and help from several dedicated family members, we were able to avoid daycare for him until he was nearly two years old. Even then, we only had to do half days and that was a conscious decision as opposed to a lack of options. We were happy to put him into full-time preschool later, even though the financial burden was difficult.

Fast forward to 2010. I was working as a High School English teacher, having just completed a Masters in Education. My wife was finishing up the last year of her medical residency while pregnant with our second son. The summer was looming and on the horizon was a new baby and a relocation of our family from Philadelphia to Virginia for my wife's first *real* job as a doctor–one that offered significant benefits over any job she could have received near our home and families. The decision to relocate was not an easy one, but it was one that we felt offered our growing family the best opportunity to be comfortable, our children a clean, safe environment to grow, and my wife's career an opportunity to start off on a very high note.

Within a month after the birth of our second son, we were in Virginia and had an important decision to make: what to do with the new baby. Our older son was starting kindergarten, so there were no issues there. Obviously, my wife staying home was out of the question. We had short-term support from my wife's grandmother, who stayed with us a few months while we transitioned, but no other family or friends to support us. We had two choices: place our infant in daycare before he could even sit up on his own or keep me home to take care of the children. After playing with some numbers, processing my prospective salary as a teacher or–shudder–a return to my previous career of retail management, we came to a mutual decision that it was best for me to stay home. It made sense both financially and in order to adhere to our belief that a child should grow up around loving family members–not paid professionals.

So, no, Miss Cashier, I don't exactly refer to it as babysitting when I am stopping off in your convenience store for an energy drink to counterbalance the lack of sleep from overnight feedings, early rising, and getting a kindergartner off to school. Would you have assumed that I was babysitting if I were a woman? No, I don't think so. But I smile, pay for my items, and struggle out the double doors while trying to let my infant not bump around too much on the way back to our car. I swallow my bitterness and accept that it isn't her fault; we men just need to demonstrate that we are both willing and capable of being the expected caretaker.

# # #

"That's a wonderful vacuum. The only complaint I have is that it's a bit heavy when carrying up steps," says a polite middle-aged woman at the electronics store. My wife and I were purchasing a new high-end vacuum for our house. I was so excited to trash the old one.

As an aside, I don't know why people complain about house cleaning devices or appliances being bad presents or demeaning to a homemaker. It's a tool that makes my job easier. Would a carpenter complain about a new drill? Would a roofer complain about a new nail gun? Would a doctor complain about a new stethoscope? I doubt it. It's not insulting; it's a pragmatic gift.

"That's okay," I replied. "I do all of the vacuuming anyway."

The woman shoots a knowing look and a bit of a wink to my wife. "Oh, he thinks he does all the vacuuming, huh?"

At that moment, I wanted to test how heavy the vacuum was by swinging it at the lady. I resisted, however, because it's not polite to hit people with vacuum cleaners in public. I suppose it's not polite to hit people with vacuum cleaners in private either, but it's certainly worse to hit a stranger in public for a comment that was not intended as an insult at all. So I bit my tongue again. I assembled the vacuum as soon as we got home so I could test it out.

The house maintenance portion of being a stay-at-home parent was probably the one I was least fearful of undertaking. Being a former retail manager, organization and cleanliness were two skills in which I had become proficient. I treated it no different from maintaining my department in a large box retailer or my small box video game store. I set up schedules for cleaning that were realistic and achievable. Let it not be said that retail taught me nothing that I could use in other elements of my life.

I am not sure why the nice lady's assumption that she had to placate the man with a verbal pat-on-the-head made me so annoyed. Maybe it was because she acted as though it was completely ridiculous that the male might be the one who handles the majority of the housework. I felt like one of those idiot men on television commercials for cleaning products, the rare time there is actually a man on there that isn't Mr. Clean or that guy on Brawny towels. "Oh, my poor husband is so dumb when it comes to cleaning stuff that I have to hold his hand and think for him."

In some ways, I actually feel that men are better suited for maintaining the household. I wash the dishes *and* fix the garbage disposal if it's broken. I wash and fold the laundry *and* replace light bulbs that are dead in the laundry room. I drive the kids to school *and* change a flat tire on the car if needed. Is this to assume that a woman is not capable of doing the latter things? Of course not. Then why is it assumed that men can't do the former? The answer is that both genders are more than capable of handling both of those. Physical limitations aside, it's silly to assume that it's impossible for one person to handle all of those tasks. One of the most wonderful things is that home repairs don't need to wait until that holiday weekend to get done. Baby taking a nap? Install a ceiling fan. Wife has a day off and takes the baby for a walk? Mow the lawn.

So while I wanted to swing our expensive new vacuum cleaner over my head to drive a point home, I held myself in restraint once again. Just like with the cashier at the convenience store, it is not this woman's fault that society views men as inept or disinterested in basic household tasks. Being a bit older than me, I imagine she *would* find it ridiculous for a man of her generation to vacuum, dust, and maintain a household. My generation and generations going forward need to dispel this misunderstanding by demonstrating that it is not ridiculous. My two sons grow up in a household where their mother goes to work and the father stays home. They need to know that, while different, our family structure is perfectly fine.

# # #

"You can't even find a job!" cried my father-in-law in the midst of a "discussion" while we were visiting family at Christmastime. Suffice to say, my father-in-law, being of the same generation as the vacuum cleaner lady, did not approve of our aforementioned family structure. This conversation stemmed from other questions about my manhood raised by my wife's father throughout the years. This was a straw-breaking-the-back type of comment, however.

"We *decided* to keep me home to look after the boys," I explained. "Your daughter is a successful doctor. Do you think *she* should be the one staying home?"

After a moment of silence, he replied, "All I know is that kids are supposed to be with their mother."

It was at that moment that I realized the real problem. He and I would never agree on this issue and continuing to argue the point was futile. He had an expectation of family structure that was thoroughly ingrained in his understanding of the world. It was not his fault; he just couldn't see past the expectations instilled in him. His mother stayed home with the kids. His dad went out and provided for the family. His wife stayed home with the kids. He went out and provided for the family. That was the cycle of life as far as he understood. This cycle led him to actually seem *disappointed* in his eldest daughter's decision to become a doctor. I felt less anger at that point and more sadness that his lack of an open mind caused such strife in our ability to have a relationship.

I was always very appreciative of my wife's parents for their support. When our first son was young, as referenced earlier, they were a huge help in keeping us from needing daycare and allowing our son to be with family instead of being raised by strangers. My mother-in-law was also very supportive of me being a stay-at-home dad. She knew it didn't mean I was a loser and just living off my wife's success. She knew that it was a hard job that required a lot of effort and that I would be doing it on an island five hours away from my previous support structures. The fact that my father-in-law didn't respect it, to me, was also a slight to stay-at-home mothers. Somehow, being a stay-at-home was not a respectful position and was okay for women but not for men. If I were a woman, I would be insulted by that concept.

"You seem to have issues with father figures," my father-in-law would add, citing my lack of accepting his advice or admonishment or whatever he felt it was.

"Maybe because I have been let down repeatedly by father figures who had issues with drugs and alcohol and were never there for me," I tersely replied.

When I found out I was going to be a father, I had one goal in mind: be a good one. I didn't know exactly what that meant, but I knew that my mother essentially raised six children—three each from two failed marriages—on her own and that addiction problems left us without reliable father figures in our lives. My own father is not a bad person. On the contrary, he's a great guy—a hard person *not* to like. He just wasn't there for me growing up. My stepfather tried to be there before addiction overtook him. He and I just never really clicked with our personalities and interests. I didn't know what it meant to be a good father, but I sure had a few examples of what it meant to be a bad one.

I came up with one simple rule to be a good father: be there. To me, being a stay-at-home father afforded me even more opportunity to be there for my boys. At the same time, I could serve as an example to them that the ideal male in today's world is not Archie Bunker from *All In The Family* or Red from *That 70's Show*, but a man that could nurture, loved to interact with his family, and support a hard-working successful woman in the modern world. While I understand why my father-in-law, who was sitting in his Archie Bunker armchair during this "discussion," couldn't understand, it still was sad to feel as though I was losing another chance at a father figure. That sadness, though, converted to determination that I could offer something different as an example to my own sons. My wife appreciates my position and she and my boys are really the only people I have to keep happy and approving at the end of the day anyway, right?

# # #

"I don't know how you do it, man," said an acquaintance through a mutual friend. This particular acquaintance happened to be a professional football player in the NFL. What he didn't know was how I managed two children on a daily basis. He told me this after he spent a day with his girlfriend and her daughter, having to look after the little one for a few hours since his girlfriend was sick. "I left the room for five seconds and she dumped half the bookshelf and emptied the trash can."

"Well, I don't know how you do what you do," I replied.

Thus went a conversation between two men who stood on complete opposite spectrums of the male career platform. He was the epitome of what it means to be a big, tough, macho guy and I was the stay-at-home dad, changing diapers and going to parent-teacher conferences. Yet, he was the one telling me he respected what I did and that he didn't think he could handle it. Talk about full-circle vindication in my ego and pride.

I always felt that I only needed the approval of my wife and my kids to feel content in what I do. My mother supported me and always has, no matter what I did with my career and life, so her approval was never in question. It would have been nice to have my father-in-law's approval but I didn't have high expectations for that. However, I felt such a swell of pride in this conversation with a guy who was practically a stranger. I think the truth of the matter is that guys really do want the approval of other men. I felt very secure in the decision to become a stay-at-home dad and, to this day, I still do. The validation I felt from the conversation with this man somehow made me feel better–like an added bonus to the security I already felt.

In my time as a stay-at-home father, I have learned tons about myself as well as the perception of gender roles in modern society. I am not a sociologist nor am I a crusader for equal rights. I do feel, though, in the same way women once forged bravely into the workplace and proved (and still are proving) they were just as capable as men, there is a counter movement of men forging bravely into

the home and proving the inverse to be just as true. I am proud to be a part of that movement and proud that there are plenty of other men taking the same steps to prove that men can be caring nurturers, primary caregivers, and competent homemakers.

About The Author

Jeremy Rodden considers himself a dad first and an author second. He is the author of the middle grade/young adult *Toonopolis* series of books that take place in a cartoon universe. He also is working on a forthcoming adult urban fantasy book series called *War of the Forgotten*. He can be found online operating his author/cartoon review blog at www.toonopolis.com or on Twitter @toonopolis.

Lastly, he is the founder/owner of Portmanteau Press LLC, the publishing company responsible for *The Myth of Mr. Mom*, his own works, and, in the future, other authors' humor and/or fantasy works.

Fang Fang Meets Super Dad

by Toby Tate

Babies are funny.

I don't just mean the fart noises they make with their lips or the way their noggins look like little bobble head dolls.

I'm talking about the way they mesmerize you with those big anime eyes and coerce you into being their slaves and buying them toys, puppies and eventually cars.

But what is *not* so funny is when you as a parent are so sleep deprived for the first few months of parenthood that you do crazy things like forget your pants and find yourself locked outside your house with no keys, or wreck your car because you thought for sure that bus was out of the way when you tried to change lanes on the four-lane freeway.

When that kind of stuff starts happening, you begin to wonder if maybe you don't have too many spoons in the soup. Working full-time, taking college classes and trying to finish your first novel, for instance, while raising a brand-new baby.

Only this baby wasn't brand-new. She was adopted from China and at thirteen months, she was already walking and even talking a little, albeit in incomprehensible Chinese baby talk. So we were not starting from scratch here. This baby already had some experience being a baby, but we had *no* experience as parents. It was a big, fast learning curve.

So we sat down one day and said, okay, is there any way we can survive on one income, at least for a while, until baby is old enough to start doing things on her own? We decided that with the cost of childcare and the fact that we were living well below our means, it made sense for me to stay home with the baby and for my wife to keep working, because, well, she was the main breadwinner. I was comfortable with that.

The only glitch was that I was a full-time student at the local university and not only the president of the honors society, but also the editor of the school paper. Since we were trying to avoid having to pay childcare, the baby would have to go along to school with me.

What an adventure that would turn out to be.

One of the first things I learned about Zoe–known at the orphanage in China as Fang Fang, pronounced "Fong Fong"–was that she was very curious. In other words, anything within reach was fair game for her grubby little fingers. That included full plates of food, beverages, small animals, noses, hair, anything made of glass, electronics, newspapers, books and especially important homework projects due the next morning. I remedied this by sitting her behind me in a chair or strapping her into a high chair and giving her a toy to play with. I considered a straight jacket, but they didn't make one small enough, so I had to ensure that she was constantly busy doing something.

I had been going to school part-time for several years and was ready to just get it over with and finish my degree. In my small town the local state university is also small and, luckily for me, quite understanding of people with children. They had granted me time off from classes to travel to China for two weeks for the adoption, for which I was grateful. I would later repay them by allowing them to know the joy of my child's presence throughout the school.

For the first few months, Zoe spent her mornings with a babysitter and I continued to work part-time. I began taking her to some of my classes when she was about two and was walking well on her own. She was also potty trained by then, so that made life quite a bit easier and less smelly. No one wants to smell a dirty diaper in the middle of history class. I made sure to bring a good stack of coloring books and a box of crayons. The girl was definitely an art lover and could draw for hours.

My classmates took an instant liking to little Zoe–so much so that when called upon to read something in class, I could rely on one of them to keep my daughter entertained temporarily. She had a habit of following me wherever I went and would often do so when I was called to the front of the class to do a presentation; she would immediately go to the chalkboard to begin playing with the chalk. That always got a good laugh from everyone except the professor. So one of my classmates would usually lean over and say, "No, no, Zoe, Daddy needs to do this by himself," and maybe open one of her coloring books and help her color a picture. It was like one big, happy family. I couldn't have done it without them.

Walking the hallways between classes was usually interesting. There's nothing like sitting in economics class and seeing a grown man suddenly stroll by with a Chinese toddler in tow. Students in the hall would either smile and say, "Aaaaaawwww," or if they were too cool for that, just ignore us like it was an everyday occurrence.

Soon, Zoe became something of a school mascot. Now it was unusual to see me anywhere on campus without the little crumb-cruncher close behind. Even my professors would see me in the hall and ask, "Where's Zoe?" I would often visit them in their offices, where Zoe would go in and begin opening desk drawers and typing on unoccupied computer keyboards. The professors thought this was cute. While I busied myself trying to restrain her, they would say, "Oh, don't worry about it. She's okay." Whose side were they on, anyway?

The biggest challenge of all, though, was editing the school newspaper with a two-year-old nearby. I wouldn't recommend it to anyone. If you are a new parent who works at home, you have my sympathies, because this probably rates as one of the toughest ways to make a living, aside from coal mining. Toddlers, especially ones who are needy, don't particularly like it when you do things that take the focus away from them. Babies who are adopted tend to have attachment problems, especially ones who lived in orphanages where dozens of other babies vied for the attention of a handful of caregivers. They are well cared for, but it's like being in a classroom with a hundred other students–you know that if you aren't persistent and don't make some kind of noise, chances are your immediate needs are going to be ignored. I'm sure that with Zoe, this wasn't the case. I am one hundred percent positive that she got plenty of attention, if for no other reason than to decrease the volume of sound emanating from her noise hole.

No, she was not shy about making her desire for attention known.

I was overjoyed when I discovered the newspaper was located in a single office space with no windows inside one of the largest buildings on campus. Since I would be working during school hours, this room would provide enough privacy so that no one would hear little Zoe if she decided to cut loose with those well-tuned vocal chords.

The problem with the office was that there were several computers with keyboards and desks with lots of drawers. Zoe was imminently drawn to these, so I learned to unplug the keyboards from the computers and lock all the desks. Eventually, she got bored with that and decided to busy herself with things I had brought for her to do, i.e. games, toys, books, puzzles, crayons and drawing pads and, most important of all, snacks. I also had to bring a sleeping bag because once she had been there for a couple of hours, she would pass out like a tranquilized monkey.

Being the editor of the paper in a university as small as the one I attended meant having to do most of the jobs myself. Though I did have a few reporters, I was photographer, sales rep, reporter, copy editor, page designer and just about everything else. It kept me busier than a squirrel in a nut factory, but I loved it. Zoe also loved it, because no matter what I was working on, she was right there next to me, watching my every move. Often, to get a closer look, she would try climbing into my lap. Then, she would try taking over the keyboard and the computer. There was just no stopping her.

I learned that the girl's attention could only be held so long by the things that Daddy had brought to keep her busy. What Daddy was doing on that big, colorful computer monitor was much more interesting. So I decided to turn on one of the computers, find a game or something that she could do on her own and teach her how to use a mouse. She was a quick learner. In the next few months, she was using the computer's drawing program and designing all kinds of things that could have been interpreted as animate or inanimate but were beautiful nonetheless.

She was quite proud of herself and I had finally attained peace.

We went on this way for two semesters. Zoe was there for the designs and layouts of nearly every newspaper I did, so I guess you could say she was my inspiration. I was working either very late at night or during school hours so even though others, like the school yearbook staff, used the office, I hardly ever saw anyone else. It would have been pretty lonely without the little tot to keep me company, in spite of her shenanigans.

When my senior year rolled around, I relinquished the newspaper job to someone else and Zoe went back to the babysitters, which neither of us liked very much. So on days when I got out of class early, she was picked up and brought home to help me do homework. My wife and I watched her grow as I continued my studies and eventually graduated at the top of my class.

When I got my first job at a "real" newspaper, it was gratifying. All that hard work had finally paid off and I was doing what I loved to do: write. I started out at the layout desk doing page design and won a first-place statewide award for a local music page that I had designed. That led to my first writing assignment as the education reporter, then as a county reporter.

After five years of getting home after my daughter went to bed, working weekends and being stressed to the max five days a week, my wife and I decided enough was enough. We didn't need the money that badly. What we needed was sanity. My first novel would soon be published and I was already contemplating my second. Writing fiction was my first love and I was, and still am, determined to make that my career. So one day I sauntered into the editor's office and said, "*Sayonara.*"

I began freelancing for that same newspaper and for several websites like eHow.com and others. I set up my office in a closet with a window that looks out into our front yard and chained myself to my chair until I eventually finished my second novel. I do like to stay in shape so I work out for about ninety minutes every day. No sense in letting my butt grow bigger than my chair, right? At this writing, there are several agents and publishers looking at the full manuscript as I work on my third novel.

More important than all that, Zoe has her daddy back–I take her to school every morning and pick her up every afternoon. I'm there for her on weekends and for her soccer practice and games. I clean the house, take care of the bills, mow the lawn and do whatever odd jobs need doing around the house. I'm here when the plumber or the electrician shows up. When my wife needs to run an errand but can't leave work, all she has to do is pick up the phone and I'm there. When Zoe's home sick from school, we don't have to call anyone, because Daddy's available.

We may not be rich and we may not be able to go on vacation whenever we want, or buy a new car or house, but we do have each other, and I'm doing what I love to do. I have a feeling that it will pay off in the long run. My wife and my daughter both have peace of mind knowing that daddy is on call 24/7.

Yeah, I think I can safely say that I have found my "stay-at-home dad" dream life; and really, I wouldn't have it any other way.

About The Author

Toby Tate is a freelance writer and reporter as well as the author of DIABLERO, a supernatural thriller published by Nightbird Publishing. He is also a musician and songwriter and lives near the Dismal Swamp in northeastern North Carolina. Check out his website at: www.tobytatestories.com.

In At The Deep End

by Leo Dee

My wife and I had discussed it at length, the old "How are things going to work when we have kids?" conversation that I'm sure everyone has had with their significant other. Laura was the university-educated one with the qualifications and salary to match whilst my job was enjoyable but less rewarding financially. From the outset, neither of us were keen on paid childcare–having someone else bringing up our baby while we're at work and missing all those special moments like first words, first steps, etc. Finally, after looking into childcare costs and seeing just how expensive it was, it seemed the ideal solution would be for me to leave work and start a new career as a stay-at-home dad.

I didn't think about it much during her pregnancy as we were both pretty consumed with the day-to-day stuff: working, buying all the baby essentials, and decorating the nursery. As such, my future job role seemed a long way away. After our beautiful daughter, Lily, was born, I was still working long hours and spending time away on business so things didn't really start to hit home until I'd left work and we all had a couple of weeks together before Laura's maternity leave ended. I'd been as hands-on as possible up until that point, but now I really had to get my head around the whole daily routine.

My new job, for my incredibly demanding little boss, started when Lily was five months old. Despite how much we'd talked about it and those two weeks of intensive training, I very much felt like I was "in at the deep end," bearing in mind we'd just made the transition from breast to formula milk, Lily was teething, and we'd begun the weaning process. There were many, many new things to consider, and I realised pretty early on that the goal posts for the daily routine were continually moving as new phases in our daughter's development began. Add into this equation the usual daily chores of laundry, washing up, vacuuming and tidying, and suddenly I had a very full day, which probably involved longer working hours than my previous job.

It was easier to keep on top of things in those early weeks. Lily loved to nap, so I'd use that time to get housework done. However, by the time she was approaching toddler status, everything went out the window as I was now spending most of my time either trying to keep her entertained or stopping her from climbing or touching something she shouldn't for fear of injury. Up until this point, I'd always assumed that those hyper little children you see running around, screaming and shouting with boundless energy were just a product of food additives and sugary drinks. That assumption was clearly incorrect; all toddlers are like this. My daughter's desire for input truly astounded me–"Read this book to me Daddy. Now read it again! I don't want to sit still–I fancy spinning around in circles and dancing till I fall over. I want to run around the house, climb the stairs, play in the garden, ENTERTAIN ME, DADDY!"

The times of easing myself into the day with a quiet cup of coffee and leisurely breakfast were gone forever. Once she's awake, she's *on* and demanding my full attention. Nap times decreased considerably and, needless to say, the daily chores list had to be trimmed and prioritised accordingly whilst I learnt vital new skills like drawing her favourite cartoon characters or making balloon animals. Getting out of the house helped. I can't really explain why, but I felt very self conscious in the early days–

something I don't think is uncommon with new dads. I heard about a guy that went to the extreme of putting "learner" plates on his son's buggy. I guess it's the natural anxiety. "Did I pack everything she needs?" "What if I need to change her while we're out?" "Is she wrapped up warm enough?" For a dad, no amount of practice or background reading can rival the mystical power of a mother's instinct. However, me feeling a bit out of my depth was not an excuse to deprive my daughter of the outside world so I quickly adopted a much needed "oh, just get on with it" approach and resolved to be less self-critical.

My newfound confidence was tested a little at playgroup. For a long time, I was the only dad there so when it came to sitting around in a circle singing songs and nursery rhymes, mine was the only deep voice in the room. This tended to pose a problem as, despite being a part-time musician, few of the songs seemed to be in my vocal range, being better suited to either The Bee Gees or Barry White with little choice for a mid-range vocalist like myself. Our daughter always found my singing amusing so I struggled on regardless. It was nice to see her interacting with the other children, playing together and learning how to share toys. I've no doubt that playgroup has helped Lily build her social skills and has made her a more confident person. For me, it was a valuable opportunity to get out of the house and mix with other parents; it's always nice to compare notes and to have those normal "is yours doing this yet?" kind of conversations.

With Laura back at work, an important part of our role reversal was to make sure that she got some quality time with Lily during the week. We're fortunate that she works fairly close to home and this ensured she could see Lily in the morning and even, in the worst-case scenario, be home in time to put her up to bed. On an average day we'll "swap over" when Laura gets home. I'll finish a few chores and make a start on dinner while she enjoys a bit of playtime and takes care of baths. I never wanted to be in a situation where Lily favoured one of us over the other, such as if she falls over, scuffs her knee and runs to me instead of mummy. I think we've managed to get the balance right, as this hasn't been an issue so far. Weekends are great as we're all together. Sometimes I'll take a step back as we're halfway through renovating our house and this gives me a chance to get on with a few of the time consuming and serious DIY jobs, of which there are plenty. Also, perhaps on more of a selfish level, it means I can have a break and recharge my batteries a little, even if it's just walking around the local DIY store for half an hour, I think it's essential to take a bit of "time out" every once in a while.

Looking back on the early days of my stay-at-home dad experience, I think I was pretty fortunate not to encounter any negative comments–well, not to my face anyway–but a few people's reactions to certain things used to baffle me a little. I was once asked at playgroup if it was me that had tied my daughter's hair that day, followed by a genuine look of surprise when I said I had. In fairness this wasn't a newly learnt skill, I had long hair for a couple of years and was already suitably proficient at tying a ponytail. On another occasion, I took my daughter for one of her immunisation jabs and the consultant commented, "So, you're looking after her today then?" to which I replied, "Yes, I look after her full time." Again, the raised eyebrow response was something to behold. Why?

One thing that really gets under my skin is when people call me a house-husband. Maybe it shouldn't bother me because, on paper, that's what I am: I'm married, I don't go to work, I take care of the house, and so on. Perhaps it's because "house-husband" is a title we don't hear often and there's no kudos or air of responsibility associated with the position. Ask anyone what a housewife is or does and the answer will inevitably be "stays at home and looks after the children." Ask the same person to define a house-husband and I doubt you'd get the same answer.

A while ago, I had to call my car insurance company to update a few details. The desk jockey on the other end of the phone went through my personal information and when he got to the "occupation" details I got the usual, "So, you're a house-husband then?" in a sarcastic voice, to which I felt the usual need to explain that I was a stay-at-home dad, thanks very much. The sarcastic voice quickly disappeared with an, "Ooh, fair play, I don't think I could do that, mate," and Mr. Desk Jockey started taking me seriously again.

Maybe it's just me. Maybe I'm just being sensitive. Maybe it doesn't matter. All I know is I'm doing a job that is primarily about taking care of my children so I'd appreciate a job title that reflects that air of responsibility, be it stay-at-home dad, house-father, daddy-day-care, non-working child rearing executive, toddler entertainment supervisor, whatever. For me, "house-husband" just doesn't cut it.

By the time Lily had reached eighteen months things were ticking along nicely. I'd found my feet and was enjoying the daily challenges of being a stay-at-home dad. Then came an addition to the story, a spanner in the works, albeit a very welcome one. Laura had previously been diagnosed with PCOS, polycystic ovary syndrome. One of the side effects of this, without going into a lot of medical detail, means it can take a while to conceive. This was certainly true with Lily and so we figured it would be a similar while before our next one. Needless to say, I was somewhat surprised when Laura told me we were expecting again!

Our son Michael's arrival into the world was a difficult one. He was born seven weeks early by emergency caesarean and spent a week in the special care unit. Thankfully, he was discharged fit and healthy, but his early arrival meant our bathroom–which I'd planned to have finished and ready by his due date–was still in mid-renovation stage, so Lily was packed off to my in-laws' and Laura and Michael spent a few days with my parents while I worked flat out to get the room in a useable state.

Another thing I've learnt along the way is our once romantic notion of restoring our period property to its former glory does not sit well with the arrival of babies and small children. I was naive in thinking that being at home all the time would mean I'd get a lot of DIY jobs done. I haven't. It's hard enough clearing the day-to-day chores, let alone finding time to re-plaster a wall or paint a room. Let's just say that after six years in our home were not quite as far along the renovation process as I'd hoped. Don't get me wrong, I wouldn't change a thing as far as our children are concerned, but living in a building site can weigh heavily sometimes.

Another parenting misconception I had was "It'll be easier the second time around." Again, this couldn't have been further from the truth. We were well prepared since we already owned most of the necessary baby-related equipment but other than that, I really can't think of anything else that was easier with Michael. Maybe it was due to his difficult start in life, but he definitely has more of a needy personality than Lily–maybe it's just a *man* thing. As with Lily, Laura breastfed Michael. For the first couple of months he'd wake every two hours for a feed but eventually we had no choice but to switch him to hungry formula, as she could no longer keep up with the demand. This proved a wise decision as his sleep patterns improved, and consequently, so did ours. Until the arrival of our children, I never fully appreciated what a precious commodity a night of unbroken sleep is.

It was interesting to see how Lily would react to his arrival. We worried there might be jealousy issues. How would she feel about this new little person getting all the attention? In short, she coped very well indeed. Before Michael was born we bought her a doll to practice with and that was an inspired idea. As with the doll, she learned to be very gentle with Michael and always keen for a cuddle. We tried to involve her as much as possible in those early stages to stop her feeling left out– for example, helping mummy get him dressed or helping daddy change his nappy. Thankfully, that approach helped keep the toddler tantrums to a minimum.

Laura has returned to work and my own personal workload has doubled. The question "How do you cope with two?" crops up quite a lot, to which I normally answer, "It's fun, but it has its moments." For me, I think that sums it up pretty well. Trying to keep them both fed, watered, rested, clean, happy and entertained is never an easy task, but then again, I didn't think it would be. They're learning to play together although it was difficult when we started bringing out a few of Lily's old toys. She was excited to see them again and, as a consequence, did not want to share with anyone.

We're making good progress though. Lily now attends pre-school for three hours every weekday, and this gives me a valuable opportunity to spend some one-on-one time with Michael. The only downside of having a happy, outgoing boisterous three-year-old sister who never stops talking is that Michael never gets a chance to get a word in. In terms of speech development, he's definitely behind where Lily was at his age, so whilst she's at pre-school we spend plenty of time reading books and attempting to communicate with each other. I'm pretty sure he enjoys this relatively quiet time and being the centre of attention for a change. I've certainly noticed how much his speech has improved over the last couple of months.

I'm looking forward to the time when they're both a little older and we can just get up, jump in the car and go somewhere without having to pack bags or worry about all the additional luggage associated with babies and toddlers. Don't get me wrong, I'm not trying to wish it all away; whoever it was that said "they grow up so fast" was definitely right. It seems like only yesterday that we brought Lily home and, before we know, it she'll be starting school full-time.

Despite all the good stuff, there are times when it's not the most enjoyable job in the world. The lack of sleep can leave you feeling like a zombie and play havoc with your short-term memory, and the sensory overload when you mix a screaming baby with a shouting toddler is really something to behold. I wouldn't change it for anything though. On a personal level, becoming a stay-at-home dad has enabled me discover a patient and tolerant side of me that I didn't know existed, and probably a person that a lot of my old work colleagues wouldn't recognise. I'm going to sound like one of those sad celebrities on a reality TV show when I say it's been "an amazing journey." I've learnt that no matter how much you read beforehand–on reflection, maybe I read too much beforehand–nothing can prepare you for the reality of parenthood. I can draw a comparison with playing in a band; you can rehearse for a gig as many times as you like, but it all comes down to what happens on the night. My wife and I read the books, did a birth plan, prepared ourselves for the non-interventional natural delivery that we both wanted. After all that, Lily was born a week late by emergency caesarean after forty-four hours labour and an epidural. Similarly, Michael was born seven weeks early by emergency caesarean after a number of complications.

I have to give total credit to Laura for having the strength to go back to work and for having the confidence in me to step into her shoes without treading on her toes, if that makes any sense. Understandably, she found it very difficult at first to be away from Lily, but I know she took some comfort in the fact that I was at home looking after her and not some hired help. Things were a little easier with Michael as we'd both been home during her maternity leave. Given the fact that he was quite a high maintenance baby, I think she was more than happy to leave him with me. Indeed, there have been a couple of occasions recently when both children have been creating havoc and misbehaving when Laura has asked me half-jokingly, "How do you cope with this every day?" We don't talk about it much, but I know there's a lot of respect and mutual admiration for each other.

I've been fortunate that our families and friends have been very supportive and this has made a tricky job much easier to deal with at times. Well, okay, maybe not everybody gets it. Some of my male friends are convinced I'm on Easy Street, but funnily enough, they're the ones who have yet to procreate!

I'm not sure how easy it is to define what I do, every parent has their own way of parenting, but if the mission statement is to raise a couple of happy, confident, well-adjusted kids, then that's what I'm aiming for; I'm also having a lot of fun in the process.

About The Author

Leo Dee lives in Kent, South East England. He left his job in June 2008 to become a full time stay-at-home dad. Up until that point, he'd spent fifteen years in the transport & logistics industry. He married Laura in 2005 and they have two children, Lily (aged three) and Michael (aged one). He enjoys music, cooking, renovating his home (when he get the spare time) and is a part time musician, blogger and tweeter who goes by the name of @DadsNursery.

http://dads-nursery.blogspot.com/

http://www.dadsnursery.com/

http://twitter.com/#!/dadsnursery

Little Pink Umbrella

by Charlie Andrews

The bus slowed in front of me, then turned left and accelerated. It continued on its course, leaving me standing in the middle of the road, arms extended in the air, flabbergasted. The sight of a six feet four inches tall man holding a little pink umbrella, complete with kitten eyes, ears and whiskers, must have evoked a bemused smirk upon anyone fortunate enough to be looking at the time. Unfortunately, the driver of the bus didn't seem to be one of them. I watched as the bus zoomed down the road, my daughter presumably onboard and safely strapped to one of the seats.

Crap.

Seven years ago, when asked if I wanted kids my standard answer was, "Maybe. No. I don't know. Kids are a lot of work." I would say it just like that every time. One should be sure, I thought, and I certainly wasn't. When I attempted to quantify it–to weigh the pros and cons–I usually ended up with a formidable column of cons. The pros side always seemed a little shorter. I had things to do, a career to build.

Every now and then, a friend or co-worker would see me play with my nieces and nephews and say, "You should have kids," or "You'd be a great father." I certainly did enjoy spending time with kids and was more than once accused of being a big kid myself. I prefer the term young at heart. So what if I like tag? In any case, the idea of being a parent made me pointedly uncomfortable. My siblings were exhausted most of the time due, at least in large part, to their kids. That much was clear; so was the look of exasperation or frustration often evident on the face of any parent dealing with raucous kids at the grocery store or playground.

That would have been enough reason to be hesitant, but what really concerned me was the fact that I would be responsible for a human. A little human that wasn't logical or smart enough to keep itself alive, let alone flourish, without guidance. I would have to be proactive in its well-being. What if it damaged itself? What if I made a mistake or wrong decision and it became damaged through my negligence? Ugh. More than adequate disincentive to reproduce in my opinion. It was a concern I couldn't push through or dismiss. So, my wife and I carried on a sort of *détente* for some number of years with her somewhere on the "let's have kids" side and me wandering around on the other.

Then the announcement: my wife must have been as apprehensive as me, not so much about becoming a parent, but about my reaction to the news that *I* would be. She gingerly waded into the cool waters of my ambivalence concerning impending fatherhood. I don't have a vivid memory of my reaction to the news. They say your memory goes out the window when you're in shock so that must be what happened. That time just fogs up like a car window on a cool fall morning. I wish I could say it was the happiest moment in my life and that I felt elated, but, truth be told, the one thing I do remember is being scared to death. I vaguely remember the urge to flee to Alaska, board a fishing boat and sail off into the North Sea. I guess I'm lucky I suppressed that urge. My wife surely would have found me. She's tenacious–in a charming way.

During my freak-out phase, otherwise known as pregnancy, the dominant theme I heard was "It's gonna change your life," and it was played by everyone. The guy bagging our groceries, security guards, doctors, nurses, old men feeding pigeons from a park bench–they all used some variation of that phrase. None wielded it so smartly as those who had made the transition: the parents. It was usually accompanied by what I would describe as a sinister little chuckle or glint in the eye that made me suspicious. I haven't any idea how many times I heard the phrase "It's gonna change your life," but I do know that it is a pathetically understated. Since when did parents become such minimalists? I now believe seasoned parents use that phrase because they are too worn out to actually describe the alteration of reality about to take place. That, and it would take a book. Rather, several books, each with the disclaimer "Results will vary."

It so happens that I had been laid off shortly before my wife informed me that our little family was about to grow. The search for a job had been suffering, partially from a lack of motivation. The news of my wife's pregnancy invigorated my effort to find employment. Responsibility was grabbing hold of my identity, and the kid didn't even have fingers or a heartbeat yet. Along with that came the realization that I would need to be secure in my new position by the time my wife began her maternity leave.

No pressure though. Tick tick tick. As B-day approached and no sign of gainful employment materialized, we began discussing "what-if" scenarios. Neither of us liked the idea of daycare; the stories of abuse, negligence, neglect and apathy were downright scary. The cost was prohibitive as well. We probably wouldn't be able to afford much more than a babysitter. No, we wanted someone invested emotionally and capable of immersing our child in a colorful, exciting environment. Someone who would develop and implement a plan to help ensure a successful child rearing process . . . so to speak. Who fit the bill? Not me, certainly, but I was available and I work for room and board, mostly. It was a matter of practicality as much as anything. And so my wife decided I would be a stay-at-home dad. I came to that conclusion about two months later.

B-day was getting closer and I began hearing phrases like "Get this thing outta me!" and "I want it out!" I also heard, often and loud, "Where's the bacon?" Bacon was one of the few things my wife could eat that wouldn't end up partially digested. It was during these times that I honed my skills in gag reflexology. Anyway, it sounded fishy to me, this bacon thing, but who was I to question? Keeping food in her was like trying to get the cat to take a pill, lots of gurgles and gagging. It all seems counterproductive to me. When nutrition is needed most, the female body wants it the least. If I were to sum up pregnancy, it means sore feet, achy back, headaches, nausea and fitful nights. My wife was feeling put upon as well I guess, but now I know this was all just the warm up. Wait till this thing comes out!

Well, it came out, as babies tend to, without any consideration regarding my feelings. We were up at 5:00 AM and were an official family three hours later. "A wondrous occasion" and "miraculous." That's what those people say. You know, the same people who say, "It'll change your life." In retrospect, childbirth is quite extraordinary. At the time, however, I was busy stressing over every tiny thing–real or imagined–that could go wrong. It was a terrifying and gut-wrenching time, until I held that baby in my arms. Then I *really* got nervous. Newborn babies are so . . . breakable.

I probably shouldn't have been allowed to hold a baby without passing a test first. They can't even hold their own head up, a design flaw right out of the chute. Maybe holding the baby *is* the test. Fail that and you don't get to take it home.

"It's gonna change your life."

It took two months for everything to settle into place and become normal. It was forever, especially compared to the bullet train otherwise known as last six years.

Now I have two kids: a son, who is six years old; and a daughter, who is four—the one who was presumably on the bus heading down the road and showing no signs of stopping.

It's not supposed to happen that way.

Nope.

Bus stops, I get on and unbuckle the tornado, I mean my daughter, and we, together, get off the bus and walk home.

The driver will see me of course.

Even though she just drove right past.

She'll look back and see the pink umbrella. I put her on the bus this morning, didn't I? I don't think that was the usual driver! She must have missed the bus.

Quickness of breath. Pitter-patter heartbeat. A little bit sweaty. Yeah, this may be panic.

Did she get sick? What, do they let just anybody drive a bus? I wish I had a cell phone; they might have tried to call.

Her teachers would never let her miss the bus, dumb dumb. I know her teachers. They'd never let that happen.

Maybe this time though. Wish I had a cell phone. Kidnapper!

Shutup dumb dumb.

That internal dialog took about ten seconds. There was more, but it was nonsensical. A car horn jolted me back into reality and reminded me that I was still in the middle of the road. As I trotted to the sidewalk, I watched the bus stop where the road came to a T, almost out of view over the hill. It started right. Stopped. Lurched left. Stopped. What the–? Finally, it committed to a right turn. It was the first time I'd ever seen a bus be indecisive. A right turn meant that the bus would make a giant loop and come back past me; there was no other way out. So I waited.

This should only take about 30 seconds.

I know.

It's been almost two minutes.

I know. There's nowhere to go down there. That bus has to come back by here.

The bus shot by in the distance heading down the other leg of the T.

Crap.

It's just coming around the other way.

Why would it do that?

It's probably taking her back to school.

Sure.

How did that bus driver not see me?

I'll wait.

No you won't. Walk home and call the school.

No. Ten minutes. Wait ten minutes.

Too long. Five.

Ok five.

I don't have my watch.

Crap.

The bus appeared, about five minutes later, give or take a heart attack or two. Two

117

minutes more and I would have been fast clipping back home to call the school. It slowed, stopped and the door swung open in front of me. A deep breath and the expletives were about to fly, and boy did I have some good ones ready.

I was standing exactly where I should have been, the only person in sight, holding a little pink kitty umbrella. Why didn't you stop and ask? Did you have to take a test for this job? Do you actually have a license or did they just find you on the street?

Of course, I didn't say any of that. I looked up at the driver. Maniacal probably best described her condition. A shock of frazzled hair stuck out the side of her head and hung limp. She furiously studied a map attached to a clipboard. I think her glasses were slightly skewed as well.

"I asked your daughter if you were her daddy and she said, 'No,' so I kept going," she rattled off in a manner that was reminiscent of her driving style. She didn't look up from the clipboard.

I shook my head. "Sorry about that." My anger was dissipating quickly.

She didn't say anything.

I unbuckled my daughter. She smiled at me. "Hi, Daddy."

"Hi, Trouble."

We stepped down and the door closed. I picked her up and asked her, "Why did you say I wasn't your daddy?"

She grinned and said, "I don't know." Then she hugged my neck.

Bill Cosby would have been proud. When I'm asked now what I do for a living, the simple answer is, "I'm a stay-at-home dad." But we know better, don't we?

About The Author

Charlie Andrews spends his days trying to tame two wild children and an ornery cat. When he's not breaking up fights or teaching the natives how to count and spell, he's building databases and fixing his wife's never-ending IT issues. In a past life, before his days and nights were ruled by two mini-human beings, he worked as a Cartographer, CAD Technician, Field Technician, Software Test Engineer and restaurant manager.

Bumming In The Margins

by Gerhi Feuren

It is a Sunday afternoon, just after six, when I start writing this essay, addressing the Myth of Mr. Mom. It is a week before the deadline and I should be polishing a manuscript, but I'm not. I'm still wondering if I'll finish this and submit. I might; I still might not.

I know that I can't do it because nothing about being a better mom than a mom makes any sense. It is a lie. To be able to write it truthfully I should first have run down the street with a placard and a burning pair of y-fronts.

Just after six on a Sunday it takes a superhuman effort to switch on the laptop and start typing. I'm typing against a deadline here–right into the margins. Keep note of those two concepts, margins and being super, I'm going to come back to them. My deadline for the moment is not for the submission of this essay, though that is looming too.

Grandma took the kids out to the park to play. They could be back in ten minutes. They could be forty minutes. I'm writing against a deadline of musical minutes. I don't know when the music is going to stop. Writing happens in these margins where a slight gap appears between life and life.

I could have had more time. But first I had to phone my wife. She is out of town for work, obviously.

"You've got time alone and the first thing you do is phone me?"

"Yeah."

"I'm touched."

We talk a bit. About life. Our lives.

Three and a half years ago we left Pietermaritzburg. Though Pietermaritzburg is the capital of KwaZulu-Natal, it is still very much a small town, with a University Campus. We went there to study further. I got up to a Masters degree until I gave up on academia. My wife got her PhD. I worked at the Municipal art museum. I had a great job, as jobs go, but I wanted to see if I can make it as a writer.

Now I'm a bad mother.

Because of the nature of this essay, I wanted to write a diatribe on the power of language and words, on how words change meanings. I wanted to say that when I write "a man" or "he" or "him," I mean exactly that: a male bastard. When I write "her" or "she" or "woman," I mean a female bitch.

Then I'd explain about vixens and cocks and why "bitch" is a compliment. I wanted to cleverly explain how either the male or the female term has become a dirty word. And how most often and erroneously the male form becomes the generic description for both male and female. And isn't it funny that for man–that is, human–it went the reverse. That man used to mean human, male and female but that it now just means male.

So that I can look smart when I come to say that there is no word for a male person who chooses to stay at home, take care of the kids and the house, and then by default works less and earns less income, if any.

There is no word for a male homemaker. Women had housewife, but I think that is now a dirty word. Home maker does not count, it is two words and insipid in it's political correctness.

But what do I want a word for?

I do not need it for the traditional man working–outside or from the house, his woman housewiving–in the house. Nor do I need it for a man where both man and woman work and share inside on a sliding scale from traditional duty-split to equal responsibilities.

I need it for a man where a woman works, outside or from home, and the man is primary householder and where said man's income is part time, infrequent or non-existent and his career can be described as being a bum.

Bum? Rhymes with mom.

Heck, I am a bum. I am not making any money. My wife runs a successful business, has high-powered meetings, signs contracts and brings home the bacon. I dabble in a hobby and make a general mess of being a good housekeeper.

The doorbell rings insistently. Grandma and the kids are back from the park. This is my deadline. I've done writing for now.

# # #

A night and a day. Monday morning. Yes, it takes hours to get back to stuff.

Today I have a full day ahead of me. The youngest has a play-date after school. The eldest: cricket and drama and then a party.

Yes, I define my business by my children's schedule.

For now I am alone at home and the only way I can get myself to write is to time myself for ten minutes at a time and sprint. It is strange that I have to devise ploys to force myself to do the one thing I really, really want to do.

If I don't, I will mope around the house all morning and not do a thing. There is a load of washing in the washroom that needs to be ironed, folded and put away. Never mind a new load that needs washing. The breakfast dishes are still in the kitchen, dirty. The house could do with a vacuum and I've only half made the bed this morning. The kids did better and made their beds, but made a mess of the rest of the room.

I have settled on bum, because it is short and rhymes nicely with mom. It also works well as a replacement–Bum's Taxi, Soccer Bum, Mr. Bum . . . Okay, maybe not that well.

The question then is, can a bum be just as good at being a bum than what a mom can be a mom?

You see, when you create a word then the question becomes stupid. Can a woman be just as good a doctor as a man? Of course she can because doctor does not imply a male or female energy.

But I am a bum. I'll never be a mom. Not even if you put me through a sex change, implant a uterus, impregnate me and get me to deliver a baby.

Okay, maybe then I'll be a mom, but inside there will be a very angry bum screaming to get out.

It is not just a matter of genetics and tools that make me what I am. There is a whole world of forces at work. And I'm okay with that. I'm a person that can deal very well with inevitabilities. I'm a good responder. Which means I don't easily take decisive charge.

Uh-oh, not such a good man then. No, my wife is much more of a go-getter, single-focus man than I am. And there are things that I'm better at than mom in the mom department–because I am not a woman. I mean, I can multi-task.

Multi-tasking as in making breakfast while marshalling the troops so that everybody reaches the table dressed and ready to eat at the same time. But then, when I do that, it is all I do. I do kitchen multi-tasking with a single-minded focus. I get in there make the chow, wash the dishes and get out.

My wife and my mother-in-law can potter for hours in the kitchen and not accomplish anything, in my humble opinion. The kitchen for me is not a place to relax and potter about in.

For a bum to be as good as a mom I think that everything needs to be rethought from the ground up.

The modern home has been developed according to the designs of the 1940s and 50s and is set around the dutiful housewife. Just ripping out a woman and plugging in a man, without any regard for the context does not make the man as good as the woman. We need an inherently different way of setting up a household when the man is the householder.

As a bum, you are at a considerable disadvantage. This bum is at a more considerable disadvantage.

We are not even living in a paradise picture perfect artistic family home with dried flowers and odd pictures on the wall. We are living in a borrowed house. The worse part of the last three and a half years is that we've been standing with our petticoats raised.

# # #

I have been attempting full time writing for three and a half years. When my wife got a post-doctoral scholarship, I used it as a get out of jail free card. We moved to Stellenbosch in the Western Cape.

Stellenbosch is her hometown. Her family still lives here. The only way we could make use of my wife's post-doctoral scholarship was to move back home, her home.

My mother-in-law lived alone in the house where my wife grew up, a big house and it was a sensible decision to move in. My mother-in-law shares the kitchen and lives in the back, the main bedroom and spare room. We took over the other bedrooms and the front of the house.

Advice? Never live with your mother-in-law.

It is not that we just share it with my mother-in-law, we also share it with all the ghosts of the past. My father-in-law designed and built the house thirty years ago. The family is invested in it with memories and yearnings. Most of the memories are still in suitcases and boxes in the garage.

We make do. I've put up a temporary wall in the vast open plan lounge in order to create a private home office. We have started repainting. We took out an old carpet and started cleaning the tile floor underneath. And every step had been a slow and arduous trek through a molasses of recriminations and adjustments.

We are lucky. We haven't fought–yet. We make compromises and we make do but as much as we try, we don't own the space where we live.

We don't live where we live.

They say you get attuned to the water of the place where you were born. I don't know about that. I know that the weather of the place you grow up becomes normal and any other weather is just not right.

I grew up with dry winters and thunderstorms in summer. Ice cold winter nights with frost and days you can walk around with a short sleeve shirt. Where winter is dry and your skin crack and summer is hot. Where, when the wind blows, you expect lightning and most likely hail and where the hail that does fall melts fast on the hot asphalt.

Now, it rains for weeks–in the winter. Rain does not smell like rain but smells like mold. And the winter can last for two months after spring equinox. When the winter rains ends, the wind starts and when you eventually get to summer, it is miserable and dry and there is never a thunderstorm to break the heat of the day.

And the washing in winter never dries.

My mother-in-law frowns on us using a clothes dryer for our laundry in winter.

Compare this: A family with children that can create a full load of washing in one afternoon. Versus one person alone, that don't dig in the dirt, don't pee in the bed, don't go to school and change clothes three times a day.

Yet, unstated, we are expected to do our washing the same way. Strangely enough, one old woman can make more dirty dishes in the kitchen than a family of four–in a quarter of the time. Pottering and accomplishing nothing?

We try and keep it that my wife takes care of meals because the kitchen stresses me out no end. But sometimes she has a meeting over lunch. Or, like this weekend, she goes away for three and a half days and then I have to go and become a kitcheneer.

Another ten minutes gone on the timer. I am now battling a hay fever attack. The weather still sucks. It is raining.

# # #

My wife finished her post-doctoral and started a business in partnership with her brother. After two years, they are making it. She only drew a full salary the last three months but has for a long time been our main breadwinner.

In the meantime, she has exhausted her savings. I've burned through my pension payout. I've maxed out on all my credit cards and my overdraft. And three and a half years later I am still seeing if I can make it as a writer.

Something always gets in the way. At first it was websites. Hand-building a website with HTML was a skill I took with me from my old job, and I enjoyed it. I felt if I could build and maintain a couple of websites for other people and if I could run a couple of my own info sites, I would make enough money to sustain myself while using my spare time to build my writing career.

Well, good luck with that.

Building websites is hard work and a hard sell. Mainly because the real work is invisible to people and they have no idea what they are paying for.

I can hand code an HTML page and get close to perfect. But then I have to say this to a client:

"I know it looks to you like I've only copied and pasted the text with some colors but no, I can not move that blue block over there. No, really I can't, unless you want to start over from scratch."

And then another month of me not doing anything else.

Worse, designing websites uses exactly the same brain cells I needed fresh for my writing.

After the first year and half I was going out of my mind. My most intelligent adult conversations happened with a three year old.

I had to get out of this place. I ended up not with one, but with two freelance projects. For the one, I curated an exhibition and, for the other, I wrote business plans and funding proposals for a start-up company within a bigger holding company.

For six months I earned a full salary and wrote nothing. The exhibition turned out a moderate success, the best part being editing and managing the publication of the catalogue.

The other project was a bust, but it still took me another year to get rid of. Here's the thing, gerbils with muskets charging through space on flying donkeys is no stretch of the imagination compared to a standard business plan.

For instance, this is just one of many conversations I had over business plans:

"So, what is the business going to do?" I am fishing here for foundation and structure on which to start drafting a business plan.

"Anything, there are some brilliant engineers here and they can do anything."

"Such as?"

"What do you want to do?"

"Okay what if we build a digital low cost and franchised community magazine published via a mobile Internet cafe."

"Sounds cool."

"So how many engineers can you commit to that."

"None at the moment."

"Writers, editors?"

"None."

"What is the budget?"

"What we pay you."

"So, who have you got to actually do any of the work for the plan I am writing?"

"You?"

All fiction you see. So I decided to stick to novels and short stories because it requires less of a stretch of the imagination. And I'm in it for the long haul.

But we took a fool path when my wife started a business at the same time as what all my income started petering out. We are now at the point where my income is virtually none.

Any money I make at the moment is by doing some book design and illustrations for my wife. Which turns out to feel quite incestuous when my wife has a choice between paying her company's bills–me–or her own salary.

# # #

I found that I possess one of the vital qualities of being a writer. I enjoy my own company. I crave being alone with myself and my own thoughts. Ironically, though I rarely get out and I infrequently talk to real people, I am very seldom alone. Afternoons, there are kids. In the morning, I share the home office with my wife, unless she is out. At least two mornings of the week, my mother-in-law potters around the house and if she isn't there, then her maid or her gardener is. Sometimes I get a chance at a Friday morning, and invariably my mom's houseguest for the weekend arrives halfway through the morning.

Oh, I don't have to converse with all these people. And they don't bother me, not like the kids. But they are there, taking up the space, breathing the air, and sucking the solitude from the atmosphere.

I feel like I am housesitting, for an extended period of time, a life sentence that is not going to end. The only thing that would have made it worse would have been if there had been any pets to take care of as well. Dogs especially, that would be the pits.

The last thing I need is to have to talk to somebody.

And yet, I joined the local business network. And I joined a speaker association. Because as an author I would or could build my platform by speaking. Except that I didn't. And the only reason I joined was the opportunity to talk to real people for a change.

My life is digital. And yet I find it difficult to forge true bonds in cyber space. I think maybe the publicness of the conversation is what holds me back. Maybe it is that I cannot natter on about stuff. Or maybe I am selfish. I don't want to listen you; I want you to listen to me.

At about this point of drafting this essay I got Jeremy's draft of the introduction of the book. "Again," I caught myself thinking, "who am I kidding? I can't write this. I'm not making it as a homemaker–I'm just a bum, hanging out at home while my wife gets the bacon."

Just the other day we discussed our current living dilemma and realised that neither my wife nor I really focus on the house. Maybe we neglect it subconsciously. Carmel Bird says you can have a fiction career or a clean house, not both. But other than my focus on writing and our luck in that nothing has really gone to pot yet, we still live with our tent pegs trailing. In three and a half years we have not settled down.

Ironically, this is the longest we have stayed at one single address in our sixteen years of marriage. We have hopped from place to place in ten months, a year, year and a half. And yet we do not live here; we have not made this our home yet; we are in a permanent state of transience, standing on the station waiting for our ship to come in.

My wife comes home from her trip with a new conviction that we need a place of our own, separate from my mother-in-law. I couldn't agree more, but I do not see myself being any help in the endeavour. I am inches away from personal bankruptcy. I can't weather any setbacks at the moment; I just don't have any money to throw at a problem.

If my car breaks down now, I'm taking the children to school on my bicycle.

Somebody said that a man gets his identity from what he does, what he earns and who he is. When you earn nothing at what you are doing, when you are doing feels like you are frolicking in La-La Land, when your identity consists of getting the kids to make their beds and folding laundry and making sandwiches and not much else, what kind of a man are you?

Are you as much a man as any other man? I am not so sure.

I ran my essay through the Gender Genie (http://bookblog.net/gender/genie.php) and found out that my writing is considered to be female. Need I say more?

About two years ago I was on the throne. Yes, I mean the loo, but run with the metaphor for a moment.

I was on the throne, besieged by supplications from my loyal subjects. As I recall correctly it was a territorial dispute. Something along the lines of:

"He looked at me."

"He kicked me."

"I don't like him."

"He doesn't want to play with me."

"What are we eating?"

"When is Mom coming home?"

You need brains to sort out these kinds of high-level negotiations–real manly stuff.

Eventually, and totally against character–I promise–I lost my temper and, without adjusting my robes, I rose from the throne and slammed the lid in righteous anger. Let it be said that I had the attention and immediate obedience of my subjects.

For about five seconds.

And I broke the lid in two.

My mother-in-law was thoroughly miffed. The toilet seat was irreplaceable. The toilet seat was the original in the house.

It was a bloody toilet seat.

I am not the king of my castle. At a matriarchal sovereign's sufferance I am merely a temporary regent, very closely watched for any signs of being a usurper.

I don't know if a man can be the mom of the house, but I do know that he needs to be the king of his own castle.

I see men around me who are battling. Men who lose their jobs. Who goes through transitions and sideways promotions. Men who get stuck and lost. I see men with wrecked marriages left, right and center and I wonder why I am lucky enough to keep mine going.

# # #

My son plays cricket and I realize I had something he will never have, an absent father. My father was a good father but a busy man.

I am one of the few dads beside the field. I have a clear sense that the other dads are there because they are sporting enthusiasts. Though I don't know how you get your sports kick from watching a bunch of six year olds fumbling with a bat and a ball. The rest of the spectators are moms, and not as many moms as there are kids. Many more of them are working stiffs, as absent to their children as what their fathers have been to them a generation ago.

I relish in the freedom I have to potter down to the sports-field and lounge on the grass and watch my kid play. But I schlep a notebook with me to the field and I make some scratchy notes for the book I'm planning.

I've got to keep my hobby alive. Except that it is not a hobby, it is a vocation. It is my career and my dream job. I am just waiting a very long time for that first paycheck.

Things are now possible that wasn't three and a half years ago. Back then it was madness giving up a job trying to make life at fiction writing with no track record. E-publishing made writing fiction a viable business; if not from the get go, then from early on.

It will still seem heretical for most but if I can stick it out for another year I think I can make it. If only I can dig in and do this thing full time.

Full time? There is the rub.

For a bum there is no such thing as full time. You only have the margins to bum in.

Let me give you a final definition of a bum.

A bum is a super man. A dedicated man that works on a dream in the margins between porridge and peed underpants. Whose every step and bit of work done is a momentous and laudable accomplishment. Who does what he does with love and dedication to his family that rivals Mother Theresa and Florence Nightingale combined.

But most of all: a humble man, daily facing a world that has no concept of understanding the world he inhabits. A world that thinks of him as just another bum.

About The Author

Gerhi Feuren has been pursuing a full time fiction-writing career since April 2008 and he is finally getting closer to achieving this despite being a bum.

Living in Stellenbosch in the Western Cape, South Africa, Gerhi shares a household with his wife and two sons, and tangentially with his mother-in-law and the generational ghosts of the last 30 years.

For his Master's degree Gerhi explored the use of role-playing games in the creation of workshop theatre.

Gerhi's website and blog can be found at http://www.gerhi.com and his Twitter handle is @GerhiFeuren.

Afterword

When I first had the idea for this project, I had unknown expectations. I had not really reached out to the stay-at-home dad community and really didn't know how many others were out there in the same situation as me. After leaving the idea in my head for a few months, I was inspired by an August 11, 2011 interview with Gloria Steinem on *The Colbert Report*.

In the interview, the feminist leader and icon said, "we know that women can do what men can do . . . but we don't know that men can do what women can do." Some people read this as an insult. A proper understanding of the feminist movement, however, is that these women, Steinem included, were not trying to flip the roles and subjugate men the way women had been for years. Their goal was to create opportunities for women to leave the home, if they so chose. The other side of the coin was to reexamine the understanding of masculinity and for men to demonstrate that, just as women can be go-getters in the world of work, men can be nurturing.

On October 6, 2011, I put out the call on my blog for submissions for this essay collection, hoping to obtain stories that demonstrated what Gloria Steinem was discussing in that interview. Within twenty-four hours, the post had been tweeted over 150 times and I had an outpouring of positive replies from other stay-at-home dads, women, and anyone else who caught wind of the project. By the aggressive deadline of October

31st, 2011, I had the eight wonderful, personal stories that make up this collection.

What amazed me personally, when reading the stories from these men, is how unique each of our situations was. While we had similarities and some crossovers, none of us arrived to our current roles from the same path. Initial response has been so positive that Portmanteau Press LLC is already strongly considering a second volume of stories for 2012 so more men can have their voices heard.

Thank you for sharing in our stories and helping spread the word that men are capable of being caring and nurturing and that the myths in popular culture about stay-at-home dads are not quite accurate.

Jeremy Rodden

November   2011